Ella Gabbai

Meditation
for Every Situation

Ella Gabbai

Meditation
for Every Situation

64 Journeys in Guided Imagination
According to the Chinese Book of Changes

Senior Editors & Producers: Contento

Translation: Kim Ben Porat

Editor: Lindsay Talmud

Illustrations: Yonat Katzir

Design: Liliya Lev-Ari

Copyright © 2016 Contento and Ella Gabbai

All rights reserved. No part of this book may be translated, reproduced, stored in a retrieval system or transmitted, in any form or by any means, electronic, photocopying, recording or otherwise, without prior permission in writing from the author and publisher.

ISBN: 978-965-550-524-5

International sole distributor: Contento

22 Isserles Street, 6701457, Tel Aviv, Israel

www.ContentoNow.com

Netanel@contento-publishing.com

Dedicated with love to my beloved Rony, who enables me to realize my dreams, and to my children, Amir, Idan and Aviv, who are the essence of inspiration.

Table of Contents

Thanks and Love 10

Preface 12

The First Try – Entering Imagination. 16

Meditations According to Category 20

How to get into a Meditative State 21

The Meditations 25

1. Celestial Inspiration 26

2. Mother Earth. 30

3. Sprouting 34

4. The Cave Story. 38

5. The Subway. 42

6. The Dove of Peace. 46

7. The Ant Nest 50

8. Improving Relationships With a Spouse 54

9. Baking Bread. 58

10. Meet Your Future Self. 62

11. Picking the Fruits 66

12. Before the Snow Melts 70

13. The Colors of Life 74

14. Gratitude 78

15. Hills of Moderation 82

16. Pamper Yourself Day 88

17. Simple Flow. 92

18. The Frogs' Song 96

19. An Ancient Chinese Saying 100

20. Journey with the Wind 104
21. The Display Window 108
22. The Hot Air Balloon 112
23. The Puzzle of My Life 116
24. New Growth 120
25. The Spring of Calmness 124
26. Energy 128
27. The Kingdom of Good Nutrition 132
28. The Chore Sack 136
29. Diving Deep 140
30. Shared Fire 144
31. The Magnet 148
32. A Letter from the Inner Child 152
33. Time to Retreat 156
34. The Room of Strength 160
35. Inner Light 164
36. Growing Towards the Light 168
37. The Tribe 172
38. The Thought Box 176
39. Gliding in a Boat 180
40. The Water Pail 184
41. Between Tides 188
42. The Emotions Compass 192
43. The Crossroad 196
44. Weeding the Garden 200
45. The Success Ball 204
46. A Message from Childhood 208

47. Connecting to the Light	212
48. The Well	216
49. The Bus of the Future	220
50. The Plate of Stones	224
51. The Calm after the Storm	228
52. The Mountain	232
53. Born Again	236
54. The Inner Vision	240
55. The Ocean of Abundance	244
56. The Market of Possibilities	248
57. A Message from the Wind	252
58. A Chat with a Good Friend	256
59. The River	260
60. Setting Limits	264
61. The Owl's Wisdom	268
62. Tidying the Room	272
63. Beyond the Peak	276
64. On the Mountainside	280
Table of meditations by type and purpose	284
Bibliography	294

Thanks and Love

I would like to extend my gratitude to everyone who helped me in the process of writing this book:

My grandmother Ruthie – who taught me that you don't necessarily have to know how to write Hebrew in order to write a book – that everything is possible!

My parents, Mira and Yaacov Miller, both of whom are natural artists. Both of them together and separately, taught me about the obligation to art of creating when it exists in your heart.

Roni, my love, who is a partner in the creation of this book in every sense of the word.

Chava Bohak, my aunt – who is always available to answer questions of grammar (and other questions).

My mother-in-law, Suzy Gabbai (an artist as well), who shared her wisdom about this book and about raising children…

To my numerous, dear friends, who supported me with their encouragement – the written page is too confining to express my gratitude for them – and for magnificent Ruthie Kolton, my sister, who was there to encourage me on this journey. I am indebted to Ravit Dominski, my writing sister, Shulamit El-Yam Berdizik, my spiritual sister, Shani Alfasi-Kakon, Yifat Solomon and Irit Tesler, friend and coach.

Deep thanks to my comrades from the Guided Imagery course, who travel with me on this journey and utilize the material presented in this book: Miri Yifrach, Efi Carp, Sharon Katzir and Anat Green.

Thank you to Natanel Semerik, CEO of ContentoNow publishing, who believed in this book: Lourdes Levy Barzili, editor; Yonat Katzir who connected me with ContentoNow – she is the most gifted illustrator I have ever met. Thanks to Rama Eshoach, editor and Natasha, producer. Thanks to Gil and Ayelet from Muse Studios, who worked with never ending patience to design this book. Many thanks to Matti Elchanati and Kim Ben-Porat for the English edition.

Yael Shafit-Garivi, Dafna and Amir Reter from Reter College, I thank you for teaching me the art of writing meditations.

A special thanks to Hadas Ariel-Paz and Edit Porat who checked all the meditations from a professional standpoint and generously gave of their knowledge in the making of this book.

I am in gratitude to anyone else who I might have left out – who offered advice and suggestions, read and commented on the material in this book.

Ella Gabbai

Even if we don't move an inch,
the seasons will still change,
in their cycles
and things around us
will happen and change.

Even if we change
one hundred and eighty degrees,
there will still be things
which remain the same.

Preface

When my son was four months old, he stopped gaining weight. The doctors began speaking of a life-threatening illness. I swung from anxiety and worries about his health to sensing that he was perfectly fine.

In the end, I was helped by my imagination. I imagined my son. I imagined him alive and well, talking and laughing at the age of seventeen. When I did this, I felt deep relief and my heart told me: "He is fine and he will be fine". Today he is four and thank God, he is healthy and he has developed according to schedule.

That experience had a deep effect on my life.

Today I am certain, from my personal experience, that imagination has the incomparable ability to heal and strengthen. The image of my healthy son was immeasurably more potent than the doctors' prognosis. With respect to medicine and science, I knew that this healthy image was stronger than all the pessimistic words from my son's caretakers. Imagination helped me exchange my anxieties and worries for belief – a belief that materialized.

As a result of that vision and my ability to connect to the power of imagination, I chose to learn guided imagery and NLP and become a professional therapist in both areas. NLP is based on subconscious communication and "reformatting" it with the help of guided imagery. During the two years of training I achieved many goals that were of utmost importance in my life.

We all come to this world equipped with gifts and one of them is the ability to imagine, to see with spiritual eyes, to hear voices, to recall feelings and smells. We can choose how we would like to use this magical gift.

Some people choose to imagine themselves and loved ones in catastrophic situations, but using the same tool, we can imagine, instead, how to protect ourselves and loved ones, how to succeed and imagine the finest, most wonderful outcomes.

The next step in my journey was to decide to publish cards called "Pictures of Inner Reflection". These cards have messages inspired by the I CHING, an ancient book of prophecy. It is a very important book in the Chinese culture, which describes 64 states of life that are continually changing, and offers ways to accommodate these changes to each situation. According to this philosophy the situations change in 8 areas: Sky, Earth, Water, Fire, Thunder, Wind, Lake and Mountain. Using coins we can assess what situation we find ourselves in and how to deal with it. This ancient practice produces 2000 interpretations, like the New Testament. I decided to present Western culture with a more accessible method, so we can learn and utilize ways to deal with our daily situations.

As time went on, and the more I worked with these cards and conducted therapy using guided imagery, I understood that the Chinese had developed a system of evaluation. Using this unique language I was able to see what situation a person was in and to offer suggestions on how to deal with it. When I understood how powerful this tool is, I decided to connect it with meditation and present the 64 situations that the I CHING lays out in its wisdom. This is how this book came into being.

This book gives you 64 healing meditations of guided imagery. We can use them to heal others or, of course, to help ourselves.

Two elements from NLP are found in the book Healing with Guided Imagery and NLP, which has the system embedded within the meditation itself alongside the wisdom of the I CHING. Together they create a powerful new tool for therapists, to group facilitators, coaches and anyone else interested in promoting growth and personal development.

I hope that every person who reads this book will find the power of healing in it and will use it to heal and endure the situations we, and our loved ones encounter.

Ella Gabbai, Yokneam, Israel – 2012

The First Try – Entering Imagination

Imagine yourself embarking on a journey...

It's a pleasant, beautiful day. Pay attention to the place you're in right now.

From here you are embarking on a journey to your desired destination.

Thinking about this creates a feeling a serenity and relaxation. It's pleasant...

Today you'll get to do something for yourself, something that will make you feel good.

We all have somewhere we desire to reach.

Today you have the opportunity to begin your journey toward that somewhere.

Perhaps it's a journey you've been dreaming about for a long time, or maybe you're setting out for a place that is still unknown, and it will reveal itself during the journey.

Are you finding it hard to begin the journey or have already begun a few times only to find yourselves stuck?

Can you imagine yourselves already arriving at your destination: where you want to be? How that somewhere looks? What sounds you hear there? What you feel being there? What you think? What you'll do once you've arrived?

Now, imagine that you have arrived at your destination. Do you encounter something on the way there, or once you've arrived that could cause you harm? Will you lose something as you head for your destination? You can check: What are the benefits of this new place? What are the downsides?

Let yourself choose the vehicle with which you will make this journey to your destination: perhaps you'll want a large vehicle, or a small one, maybe you want a big trunk because you want to take things with you and maybe you only want to bring a few things on the trip or that you believe whatever you need will be available to you as you travel. Let yourself choose the perfect car for your journey, the one that will take you to your destination. You get into the car. Have a seat. The journey has now begun – peek out the window and pay attention to the scenery: Is it scenery you like? What sounds do you hear? What is the temperature like in the car? Is it pleasant? Is it hot? Or cold? Feel your body settled in the seat. The journey calms you, there's something about movement that puts you at ease. While you move you can note the traffic signals on the way to your destination: Maybe there are signs? Or perhaps markings on the road? Perhaps you stop and ask for directions. Perhaps you've brought along a map that shows you the exact route? Or even a GPS?

Look at the scenery – does it change as you travel? Is something changing within you? Feel free to stop for fuel. You will see a gas station any second now and will be able to stock up on what you need for the journey: energy, courage, flexibility, open mindedness and anything else you feel might help you on your journey. Take a moment for yourself and choose how will re-energize yourself with exactly those things that suit you.

You continue your journey – headed towards your destination.

You stock up on things that will help you to move forward, and perhaps you will use them in the event of an obstacle. Check: Is there something bothering you on your way? Is there something on the road? Are you feeling it hard to move forward? Perhaps something is holding you back? Allow yourself to discover what will come to your aid so you will be able to move forward and see if anything you got at the gas station can be of help.

Check to see what keeps you where you are and doesn't let you move forward, making the transition difficult. What happens in the places where you feel stuck? What are the sounds you hear there? What do you feel? How do you behave? What thoughts run through your head?

Some of the obstacles on the way are external and some from inside you: fears, doubts, past attempts.

You continue to move and move forward. You've already come a long way and you begin to feel like you are getting closer to your destination. You are traveling at a speed that suits you, and now you see your destination in the distance. Very slowly, you get closer to it, you'll be there very soon, in moments you will arrive and now, you are here.

Examine your destination: How does it look? Does it look as you imagined? Are the sounds what you thought they would be? How do you feel now that you are here? What thoughts run through your head? What are you doing? Sense the ability to reach your goal in the way that suits you, at your own pace, transported in the vehicle of your choice and allow yourself to be there – in the place where you have arrived.

Meditations According to Category

Exercising our imagination allows us to create a desired and attainable goal or a path – including the experiences within the exercise. I chose to divide the meditations in this book into five main categories. This division makes it easier to choose the best meditation for each situation.

1. Meditations into the Past – The first category of meditations is connected to our origins. When we move towards our goal, we go equipped with all our experiences, beginning from childhood. Our past molds how we manage our present and future. So, this first group of mediations refers to our past. These meditations can strengthen our positive experiences and learn how they can serve our present and future.

2. Meditations into the Future – After we have decided to venture into our journey, we want to travel to the destination we set as a goal. That goal can change as we travel, though the image we create in the future remains our objective. These meditations lead us into that desired future, and I believe that the image of an optimal future is worth a thousand words!

3. Meditations to Fortify Resources – We are all equipped with resources: bravery, intuition, faith, hope, self-love and more. Even with all these resources, we must continue to add resources now and then, to fuel up, and remember our abilities and resources.

4. Meditations for Problem Solving – If a vehicle breaks down, we fix it, and so too, can we repair things that have gone astray. These meditations "fix" problems and clear obstacles that may appear in our lives, improving our ability to work on them (just

as a mechanic works on cars), in order to continue our journey to the desired outcome.
5. Meditations to find your Direction – If we lose our way and realize that our journey is not right for us, these meditations help us assess the situation anew in order to change direction if needed and chose what is right for us and one that the heart desires.

How to get into a Meditative State

Meditating is a practice we acquire.

All of us experience events that are difficult to handle and often it is hard to break free from their grip. When we meditate everything is alright – even if our mind is busy thinking about our affairs when we begin meditating. The principle is simple: the more we meditate, the more we are able to release intruding thoughts.

Even if we "disappear" or fall asleep during meditation, it's fine. It means we were able to allow ourselves to rest. During meditation, the subconscious mind receives all the messages that are important to hear, even if we weren't fully present and even if we simply entered a state of relaxation and serenity.

It is important to emphasize that there is no wrong way to meditate. Everything that happens during a meditation is okay!

How to Practice the Meditations in this Book

There are a few options:

You can ask someone to read the meditations to you. You can also record yourselves reading the meditations. You can also simply lie down and read the meditations, occasionally closing your eyes and imagining what you have just read.

Certain people, children in particular, can usually practice meditation with open eyes.

You can also record the meditations and listen to them before you go to sleep, continuing to listen while you sleep.

Reading the Meditations to Others

The meditations in this book are suited to different situations.

For those who want to help people or are practitioners wanting to guide their clients through a process of evolvement the questions is how we decide on the suitable meditation.

Another way to decide is to use my Meditation cards, "Pictures of Inner Reflection".

I also suggest talking with the client and trying to assess his or her situation and then the suitable meditation. You can begin with assessing which category of meditations is applicable at the moment.

Before meditating find a place to sit or lay down, dim the lights, light a candle and play music that feels right for you. It is important to feel serene and peaceful.

Three dots (...) in the meditations enable moments of rest before continuing. When more than a few seconds of rest are needed, it is stated in the meditation.

If the facilitator or friend falls asleep during the reading of a meditation and doesn't wake-up when it is done, call him or her gently by name. If he or she still doesn't wake up then touch them gently on the shoulder and say their name again.

Usually everyone wakes up at this stage.

*The Meditations**

As you read the meditation,

You can make it longer or shorter...

You can slow down or go faster...

You can follow the text or improvise...

And let the power of imagination lift you away,

With ease, to somewhere else...

Better...

*The names for this technique are: "Meditation", "Imagination" or "Trance". In this book I have chosen to use "Meditation".

1. Celestial Inspiration

Category:
Problem solving

Who will benefit from this mediation?
Whoever wants to connect with the power of creation within himself/herself and magnify it.

The power of creation

Accept the gift of this moment:
The powers of creating, inspiration,
Energy and ability – they are all
Available to you now.
This is the beginning of a
journey to who
You were meant to be.
What you create now,
Will be the foundation
For things you will encounter
Later.

Find a comfortable position... you can feel your body against the mattress or the chair... take a deep breath and allow yourself to slowly relax... you can relax every part of your body... listen to the sounds from outside and those around you... in this room... listen to the music... feel the temperature of the room... take a few more deep breaths... with every breath your body serenity flows through your body... a feeling of relaxation and comfort washes over you...

Now you will be able to imagine yourself in a quiet place in nature, sitting on a large rock, looking at the sky... sky the color of light blue... endless skies... white clouds in all kinds of shapes... you relax while you look at the sky and are filled with a sense of serenity... the clouds form shapes that you like... perhaps they resemble animals... or other shapes... the sky and the clouds create a sense of comfort...

Next to you... very close... flows a river... the place is beautiful... you look around you... at the clear blue water flowing and the sky above you... there's a smell of... freshly cut grass... this is a special place... full of inspiration and magic... the sound of the water flowing is a magical melody for you... this place looks like a wondrous drawing... there is a special feeling... the feeling of being inspired... something is going to happen... something that will bring with it a change for the good... you are relaxed and peaceful... like the water in the river... the sense of serenity deepens within you...

A kind, old man arrives... he invites you to take a walk around this special spot... you follow him... breathing in the scents of nature... taking note of the things you see on the river bank... there is a comfortable easy chair, soft and inviting... and on it is a pad of paper... it calls you to write something down... not far from it is a painter's easel, next to it brushes and paints... a canvas sitting on the easel... not far away are musical instruments... different sized drums... a piano... violin and saxophone... and many other musical instruments... close by is a sign that says: "Here anything can be created..." there are large cubes and tools, all kind of materials, pipes and pieces of wood... rolls of paper for sketches... and many other things to help whoever wants to create something...

One spot awaits you, and you can decide how it will look and what you can create there... a spot that suits you perfectly... where you can build anything you dream of... without being disturbed... without limits... you examine the different options... the old man explains that anything you create here will come out exactly as you plan... here you are free to create exactly what you desire... you feel calm and protected... filled with inspiration... you know anything you create will be received with love... everything is possible in this special place... anything you have ever imagined, can be created now...

You try out the different spots... then choose one... you have all the time you need... you have enough time to create what you desire...

I will be silent for two minutes and give you time to make your creation... you will hear my voice again in two minutes...

You have created something new... something that you have wanted to create for a long time, and now, you have had the place and the time... the old man smiles at you... he leads you to a secret place under a tree... this is a place where you can clean yourself from any feelings of criticism about your creation... where you can erase any doubt... you can lean on the tree and deposit your feelings of criticism and doubt at its trunk... as if they have been a load on you up until now... you like what you've created... and you know it will lead you to the future you have imagined... you are invited to take a token of so that you will remember the rare ability you have to create wonderful things... special things... as special as you...

The old man leads you back and invites you to use any of the spots you like... here you will always be able to create anything you desire with ease and joy... more and more... to create your destiny... with a sense of satisfaction and sureness you say goodbye and begin the journey back...

On the way you look at the river and see a beautiful drawing in it... the drawing of a master... the river reflects the sky and willowy clouds... the clouds make a beautiful design in the water... special beyond words... you look at the picture that nature designed and are filled with joy from the ability to create that is inherent in everything...

With this wonderful feeling you begin to return to the here and now, to this room... slowly, slowly... feel your body and the temperature of the room... move your feet a bit... gently, at your own pace... when you are ready open your eyes... and return to regular consciousness... awake... in the here and now.

1. Celestial Inspiration

2. Mother Earth

Category:
Problem solving

Who will benefit from this meditation?

Whoever wants to get pregnant and/or connect with her sense of motherhood, for whoever wants to connect with her tender, feminine side and to allow things to develop on their own.

Endurance

*Like Mother Earth
let yourself endure, be lead
and accept what takes place.
Take time for yourself and
accept things in faith and
serenity without trying to
influence them.*

A llow yourself to find a comfortable position... feel every part of your body feel relaxed... take a deep breath... feel the temperature in the room... and let yourself relax slowly, slowly... take another deep breath... listen to the sounds outside... and the sounds in the room... to the music... the music and the sounds accompanying you as you relax... letting you rest... to take into you, to let go... pay attention to your breath... to the rate you are breathing... does the air come and go with ease...? Paying attention to your breath calms you more and more...

Imagine yourself standing on a small hill, looking into a valley... it's a beautiful day and a spring sun is shining... you look around and see that the valley is full of greenery and the sky is blue... rows of flowers decorate the valley in yellow and pink... you hear the sound of baby birds on a tree nearby... their mother brings them food and they chirp happily... you feel a soft breeze on your face and the warmth of the sun on your skin feels pleasant... you feel the earth beneath your feet... calm and relaxed you begin to walk towards the valley...

As you go down a path you smell flowers and freshly cut grass... you inhale the pleasant smells and feel a sense of comfort quietly washing over you... you continue making your way down with serenity and sureness... enjoying the spring view...

From afar you see a tree with something beside it... you slowly approach... and observe... there, next to tree, lie a colorful blanket and pillow... when you get even closer you see that your name is embroidered on the little pillow... this place has been waiting for you... you bend down and then lie on the blanket... putting your head on the soft pillow... you lie comfortably... feeling the soft earth... its warmth... the tree shading you from above... the pleasant sun gently warming your body...

Let yourself feel the earth completely... to feel your closeness to Mother Earth... to enmesh with her... lying on the earth allows you to feel the quiet within her... sense her comfort... the earth is simply there... in peace... allows everything to come to her... allowing the tree to provide shade... the sun to warm her when she's cold... allows everything to happen within serenity, naturally. She simply is...

And like the earth, let yourself be tender and accepting... let the seeds from the flowers reach you... at their pace... be available and accepting of them... let the next rain water them... the sun to shine on them... and you, simply be present for them... allowing them to sprout next to you...

The earth changes and evolves according to nature's cycles... it simply responds with sensitivity to what happens... it knows how it heals itself... it simply responds to what is happening... adapts... you lie on the earth and feel how its characteristics move into you... you can also lie still, knowing that the world is moving at the right speed... everything happening when it should... you are simply here to receive... to contain... to welcome what's happening... you are simply present... open and allowing for things to come to you...

I will be quiet for the next two minutes. This is the time to accept the healing message of Mother Earth... you will hear my speak again in two minutes...

Now you are feeling great relief... you've rested and gathered strength... you've learned something about the ancient wisdom of Mother Earth... now you can awake... slowly and start to move back onto the hill...

and as you walk up... see that many hours have passed while you were lying on the ground... soon evening will come and the sun is already sinking... feel rested and calm and peaceful as dusk arrives and you slowly return to the hill where you stood before...

Now, with this deep sense of peace and new awareness that you received from Mother Earth you can return to this room... move your hands a bit... then your legs... take a deep breath and allow your body to wake... slowly... slowly... you can return to your regular state of wakefulness, gently... at your own pace... can open your eyes... and return to the here and now.

2. Mother Earth

3. Sprouting

Category:
Strengthening of resources

Who will benefit from this meditation?
Whoever is experiencing uncertainty, fear and excitement on their way to a new path.

Difficult beginnings

*You are feeling confused,
because something
Inside you is asking to change
and evolve towards
a new path.
New things can be frightening
Because you're not sure where
they will lead.
Concentrate and focus
on yourself.
Claim knowledge you own
that can help.*

Allow yourself to find a comfortable position... feel your body on the sofa, chair or mattress... you are resting and slowly feel relaxed... this your rest time... for your body... this is the time when you can let your mind rest from its thoughts and let go... you can hear the sounds outside... let yourself focus on my voice... and feel how the peacefulness fills you... you are comfortable and at ease more and more minute by minute...

Imagine yourself as a small seed resting on soil... you can choose: this is the seed of a fruit tree, a bush or a flower... the seed on the soil is gently surrounded... it has everything it needs from the soil: nutrition and water... comfort and warmth... all this surrounds it in calmness and ease... a pleasant darkness surrounds the tiny seed; it sees only dimly and hears only soft voices from outside that are far away... it feels safe... and sends roots down into the earth... roots which can nurture it perfectly...

Slowly and gradually, the seed begins to sprout... it wants to send a stalk up and out of the ground... into the world... to see what's going on outside... to hear the voices clearly... to feel the wind, rain... to breath the fresh air... it knows it has something of worth to offer the world... and it wants to leave the womb of Mother Earth and to move up and out...

You too, like the seed, feel a longing to move forward... to see new things... to hear more sounds... to feel new things... to smell new scents and to taste new tastes... you too, like the seedling... feel the need to move forward... perhaps this is scary at first to move from the familiar place... but still, you have a strong urge to do it anyway... you feel this is the time to make some changes... you are just like the seedling that wants to push up and out of Mother Earth...

Though something is stopping it from coming out. It tries to push its stalk up... but the space is blocked... something heavy is there and it tries to move it... a thin, delicate stalk but it tries to move it anyway... the stalk stops in order to gather strength from its efforts... it feels sad, because it wanted to branch out of the earth and into the world above... it checks to see how it can do this... it looks at other seedlings and sees that they are trying to move upwards... something is holding them back...

It continues to grow higher... to grow higher... to the place where it will be able to break out of the earth and breath fresh air... it encourages itself, gathers courage, a feeling of ability, bravery and confidence... it adds inch after inch to itself... it curves and pushes and starts to feel better, then tries again to push out into a new place... slowly and gradually... it grows more and more... it's still hard for it to break the earth... it is stronger and longer... another try and then another... it doesn't give up... it is stronger and longer, then finally it is able to bypass the blockage... and sprout up out of the ground...

It comes out into the light... into the air... the sun's rays happily receive it... it gets used to the sun for the most part... the world around it is beautiful... soft grass grows... a pleasant aroma comes from it... the stem hears gentle sounds from the grass around it... a huge patch of blue sun above it... butterflies fly around beating their wings... it feels a deep happiness that it was able to sprout from the earth... pride that its efforts succeeded... next to it is a rock from beneath which it managed to escape. It sees what its obstacle had been... the small stem is happy that it found a different way to break through and grow...

it continues to grow and becomes a tree... or a bush... or a beautiful flower... one of a kind... from day to day its ability to find its way to be brave in every situation... a feeling of ability, courage and sureness.

You are exactly like the stem – growing stronger and stronger every day... succeeding in dealing with every situation... even if the beginning looks difficult... you are able to overcome... to continue moving forward... to evolve and grow...

So, with this amazing feeling of strength, you slowly begin to come back to the here and now, to this room... move your hands... then your feet... pay attention to your breath... you will be able to sense when your body is fully awake, your breath speeds up and your body feels refreshed after a rest... everyone at his or her pace... slowly open your eyes and come back to the here and now.

3. Sprouting

4. The Cave Story

Category:
Strengthening Resources

Who can benefit from this meditation?
People who are interested in developing new coping strategies and in learning how to request and accept help from others.

A new experience

*Things might be looking a bit complicated right now.
This is only because
you haven't been in this
particular situation before.
This is an opportunity to grow
and evolve.
Seek guides who are familiar
with this path
and ask for their help in
order to move forward.*

Allow yourself to find a comfortable position... for every limb in your body to feel comfortable... and take a deep breath... feel the temperature of the room... allow yourself slowly, slowly to relax... listen to sounds coming from outside... and the sounds in the room... to the sound of the music... let the music and my voice lead you into relaxation and rest... take it all in and relax... slowly, slowly... pay attention to your breath... the pace of your breath... does the air come in and out with ease? With every breath comes more and more serenity and calm... with every exhalation, let go of what you don't need... stress, worries, pressure, anxiety... take another deep breath... breath regularly... paying attention to your breath calms you more and more...

Imagine yourself walking through a large green park on a clear autumn day... the skies are clear and white clouds float above... you look at the clouds and find interesting shapes in them... your surroundings... soft green grass, all types and sizes of trees... some of the trees are shedding their leaves onto the ground... and some have leaves that stay green in autumn... there are paths in the park that lead in different directions...

This is your first time in this park and you are excited to discover beautiful paths... to see different sights and hear different sounds... to feel the fresh air... to smell everything... you choose a path and start walking downwards... the sound of dried leaves crunching under your feet... a feeling of serenity fills you... the peacefulness of a restful walk...

You move forward and continue down the path and then onto other paths that branch out from it... the clouds move with you... their shape changes... the path is pretty... birds chirp to greet you... rare flowers are growing on the side of the path and you stop and look at them... different kinds of animals cross your path and look at you... your mood is calm... you feel pleased...

After a while, you decide to make your way back... you turn around and take the same path back but find yourself at a place that looks completely new... you understand that you've lost your way... but you're not upset, just curious about your surroundings and try to find clues that will lead to the right way... you see that there is a cave to your right... an old woman with kind eyes smiles at you and invites you inside... you look at her... she seems familiar... maybe it's someone you know... or that you knew once?

You decide to go into the cave, to sit inside and rest... the old woman remains at the entrance... you feel secure and safe... the tunnel receives you with a dark and pleasant coolness... you're tired from walking and are happy to sit and rest a while... sure that you'll find your way in a bit... you are happy to discover that this is a special tunnel... a cave where you can ask questions and get answers from within yourself... you ask the cave the way back and you receive the answer in the echoes... you know there is someone outside who will lead you... someone you can count on... someone who believes in you and watches over you... you are filled with new energy... you remember similar situations that you handled successfully... you know that this time you'll be able to find your way... there is strength in you... you leave the cave... thankful that it reminded you that you can ask it for advice, as well as from others and from yourself.

You are outside again and see that it rained while you were in the cave... the clouds above you are now gray... the wet air from the rain fills you with a feeling of newness... the wise old woman is still standing at the opening of the cave... she smiles and gestures that she can lead you back... you walk next to her and she leads you towards the park's entrance... you walk to where you began your expedition... thinking about how you'll be able to manage new challenges successfully... now filled with a feeling that you can always turn to those who know the way and they will come to your aid... every experience allows you to become stronger, to grow and evolve... you say goodbye to the woman and thank her for her help... and here you are... you've arrived at the edge of the park...

And with this knowledge, you are filled with a new sense of strength... when old-new abilities are awake within you... you are now invited to return... at a pace that suits you... to this room... you slowly begin to return to everyday consciousness... to feel your body again... you move your hands around a bit... and your feet... you open your eyes and return... at your own pace... to here and now.

4. The Cave Story

5. The Subway

Category:
Strengthening Resources

Who can benefit from this meditation?
Anybody who is forced to wait for something that cannot possibly happen immediately.

Waiting

*Nothing is moving now,
so all you can do is wait.
Wait until circumstances
are right for action.
Utilize the waiting time
to think about the situation
and to explore the right way
for you to act.*

Allow yourself to find a comfortable position... for every limb in your body to feel comfortable... listen to sounds coming from outside... and the sounds in the room... to the sound of the music... let the music and my voice lead you into relaxation and rest... take you inside yourself and relax... take a deep breath... and another deep breath... and return to a regular breathing rhythm... you will be able to pay attention to the rhythm of your breathing... does the air come in and out with ease? You will sense how paying attention to your breathing calms you more and more...

Imagine yourself on a clear, pleasant day standing in a square in a beautiful city... it is an ancient city, with well-designed buildings... buildings like they used to be, large and pleasant... people are slowly walking along wide sidewalks... all is calm... the sounds of the city fill you with pleasant feelings... you know that today you are about to embark on a very special journey... a journey on the subway of this special city...

You begin to make your way down the cobbled street... the sound of your steps echoes on the sidewalk... the air is cool and pleasant, the walk calms you... it allows you to shut yourself off from the sounds of the city... at the bottom of the street you can hear cars travelling... people are chatting... on your way you look at the store windows... and enter the gate leading to the subway, full of expectation...

You are about to travel to a place you have wanted to get to, for a long time... now you have the opportunity to do so... you buy a ticket and you know that the journey will take a long time... but it does not bother you. You have the feeling that during the journey you will experience affirmation and encouragement... you go down the escalator and find yourself among people... the tumult of the subway... however, you are calm and relaxed knowing that you are going to a destination that is so important to you... you stand and wait for the train... trains pass... some stop, some don't... your train has not arrived yet... you wait calmly knowing that your train is bound to come. Soon it will reach the station... to fetch you...

It does indeed arrive and stops right next to you... the door opens and you get in... in the carriage there is a vacant place next to the window and you sit down... the train begins to move and you look out of the window and see the color of the wall of the tunnel... the train is going to go through many tunnels... and in every tunnel you will have something that helps you to pass the journey in the nicest possible way...

The first tunnel is your self-confidence tunnel, and it is blue... it allows you to become stronger and receive strength... you sense that your self-confidence is about to be upgraded... your whole body is enshrouded in blue, and with it, greater confidence... you inhale this feeling of confidence. It fills you up... instilling you with calm and relaxation... in the tunnel your confidence is growing from minute to minute... (wait a little).

The train leaves the blue tunnel and enters a beautiful yellow tunnel lit up by a bright light... this is the tunnel of courage. The abundance of yellow light fills your body with the feeling that you have the courage to do anything and to succeed... this feeling fills your body... you breathe in the courage and fill your whole body with courage... with bright yellow light... the feeling of courage creates a calming comfort in you... (wait a little).

Now the train is leaving the yellow tunnel and entering the red tunnel, the tunnel of love... the red light lets you fill yourself up with love...

the love expands from your heart and washes you with a good, soft, reddish light... you feel love for yourself... for members of your family... love for friends... love envelopes you and caresses you... (wait a little).

Finally, the train leaves the tunnel of love and enters the last tunnel of the journey... the orange tunnel, the tunnel of your intuition... in this tunnel your ability to sense exactly what is right for you in every situation will become greater... orange light gradually fills your body... flows inside you... you sense that the orange light, together with the knowledge that you can rely on your intuition relaxes you... giving you defense and strength... the train leaves the orange tunnel and will reach the final destination in about two minutes.

I will now be quiet for two minutes, in which you will be able to experience all the colors that have filled you... the blue, the yellow, the red and the orange... feel the self-confidence, the courage, the love and the intuition... and be thankful for the empowering journey you have been on... you will hear my voice again in two minutes...

The train reaches the last station and stops... you get up from your place and leave the train with the feeling that the journey filled you with much strength and ability... you leave the station and begin to stride upwards in the direction of the city in the joyful knowledge that you can always return to the subway and refill yourself with strength...

Now, slowly and gradually, you can return to here, to this room... you are invited to stretch your feet a little... and your hands... you let your body wake up gradually... take a deep breath... and at your own pace you can return to full awareness, to open your eyes and to return to the here and now.

5. The Subway

6. *The Dove of Peace*

Category:
Strengthening Resources

Who can benefit from this meditation?
Anybody who is experiencing anger towards someone or is involved in a conflict or argument and wants to examine the situation in order to arrive at a solution.

Conflict

*At the moment there is a resistance that does not allow you to develop.
You are convinced that you are right and this only makes the situation worse.
It is preferable to take a step back and concede, a head-on confrontation does not advance the development you are seeking.*

Find a comfortable posture... you will feel the contact of your body with the mattress or the chair... take a deep breath and let yourself calm down slowly... relax all parts of your body... listen to the sounds coming from outside and those around you, here in the room... pay attention to the music... sense the temperature of the room... take a few more deep breaths... With every breath calmness spreads around your body... the feeling of calm and comfort fills you...

And now, imagine if you were a dove perched on the top of a tree... it is a tall, broad tree, with green leaves... and the dove is standing looking at a wide valley... each of you is now a white dove, perched on a tree looking around... you can hear the gentle rustling of the leaves in the wind... the pleasant sound relaxes you and you feel calm in the tree... you can feel the air currents blowing around you and caressing you... under the tree there is a little lake... you look at it and you hear the trickle of the water...

Soon you will fly to the valley... in the meantime you look at the view spread out at your feet... carpet upon carpet of amazing colors and hues: dark green... light green... pale yellow... brown... fields spread out all around... from here you can see everything, enjoy everything, get excited and remain calm and relaxed... and you are indeed calm and relaxed... at the same time you yearn to fly and observe closely what is going on in the valley...

You start to fly... knowing that today you will reach new insights with regard to the person with whom you have an argument or confrontation... pay attention during the flight – what thoughts arise about him/her... what do you feel about this person? Connect well to yourself and feel what is going on inside you... what happens to you when you see him/her and are reminded of your relationship, the tensions that exist between you... what thoughts and feelings arise?... you fly above the valley and begin the descend... around you is a white cloud mist... you go through the mist... for a moment you are surrounded by mist... a white, pleasant and soft cotton wool enwraps you all over and relaxes you... you pass through the cloud mist and return to the sky... below you see buildings... it is a small village...

You look down... suddenly you see the person with whom you are in conflict... you fly lower and lower until you reach the person... and you feel that in a moment you are going to actually become that person... you will be able to enter his/her character and body... you fly lower and look, it happens – you enter his/her body and become him (or her)... and now, allow yourself to see the world through his/her eyes... to feel like him... to move like him... to think like him... to behave like him... what are his intentions?... what motivates him?... what does he think and feel?... how does he see you, and what does he think about you?... why does he behave the way he does with you?...

I will now be quiet for two minutes to allow you to fully enter into him... you will hear my voice again in two minutes.

And now you can gently and tenderly leave the person's body... and return to being a dove... let yourself feel like a dove that passed by chance... and it watches everything that is happening from the outside, as all this does not concern it... it concerns people, not birds... what, in your view, does the dove see? What does it understand of the situation?... what can it see of the proceedings from its bird's eye view? Wait a moment... according to the dove, what can change and perhaps improve the situation?... what does it say?... what can it suggest to you so that both sides will feel easier? (wait a little)

We looked again from on high... you can sit on a tree top or on a roof and listen in silence... look at everything from above, from afar... afterwards you can go back to being yourself just as the dove went back... to go back to your stance... you will be able to see what has changed... do you feel different?... are you thinking differently?... will you want to change something in your conduct towards that person?... what seems best?... there should be talk.

I will now be quiet for one minute to allow you to experience the future change, to see what new sights appear... what feelings arise... you will be able to hear my voice in one minute... and you start flying in the sky...

On your way you pick an olive branch... symbol of the peace that you will start to bring to your life... slowly, slowly you return to your tree... you pass through a screen of misty cloud... you fly higher and higher... until you reach the tree... you will be able to keep the insights you gained from this bird... the special sense of looking afresh... and again, you are perched on the tree... and again you are looking at the little lake below it...

And with the insights from your magical bird, and with these feelings of moderation and relaxation, slowly, slowly and gradually, you begin to return to here, to this room, to your life, your body... you can move your feet a little... and your legs... move your body gently... move your head gently from side to side... take a deep breath... and another breath... slowly open your eyes and return at your pace to normal wakefulness... to full awareness... and to here and now.

6. The Dove of Peace

7. *The Ant Nest*

Category:
Problem Solving

Who can benefit from this meditation?
People seeking to increase their ability to achieve goals through teamwork and unifying forces.

United force

*Take a moment be alone in order to prepare for your need to be together.
Afterwards get ready for action in a group.
This has the power to set in motion processes that are important to you.
The group will also protect you in a time of need.*

Find a comfortable posture... close your eyes and allow yourself to focus your attention on your head... sense how it feels from inside... relax the head, notice how pleasant it is to pay relaxed attention to your head... and now you can travel around your whole body with the relaxed attention... slowly, slowly and tenderly... sense how much it relaxes... perhaps you can hear sounds coming from outside or from inside the room... these sounds and the music playing help you to focus your attention on all the parts of your body... down to your feet... and when your attention reaches your feet, you are already relaxed and calm...

You are standing at the start of a mysterious path... it is a pleasant summer day... warm and pleasant... there are low bushes on either side of the path that exude a pleasant scent and you sense that this path, because of its special qualities can lead you to something new... you look around you and at your feet on the path you notice lots of small, black ants walking in a line... you sense that the ants are calling you to follow them...

You set out after the black ants... they march along the slope of the path... your striding behind them, at their pace, calms you... you can even hear the rustle of their tiny legs... on their backs they are carrying grains that they are bringing to their nest... you sense the ease of their little steps... their certainty of the way... they reach the large ant nest... you sit down next to it and observe... lots of ants are going into and out of the nest...

One ant approaches you and invites you to go on a tour of the nest... it radiates friendship, tenderness and good will, though you are doubtful – how will you manage to enter?... however, the good ant has thought of everything... it gives you a potion to drink... you trust the ant and know that the potion with help you... it shrinks you to a size exactly like that of the ant... and now you can enter the nest... you march behind the ant... and now all the ants are as big as you are... the ant explains to you how they operate... you follow the ant into the nest and within a few seconds your eyes get accustomed to the dark... you hear the sound of work in the nest... it looks and sounds like a factory... the ants operate in a group... the rules are simple... and all of them work together towards a common goal...

Inside the ants have built long, convoluted tunnels... just like a miniature palace, full of branches... they go out to bring food... this is a difficult task when trying to do it alone... though in a big group the ants can obtain enough food... and even store food for the winter... the ant guides you through the burrow and shows you the role of each of the ants and how they communicate with each other by means of the trail they leave behind them... that is how they know where there is food...

There is quiet communication among the ants... each one knows its role and they enjoy working together... when you think about the work the ants do you are filled with the sense of an ability to collaborate with people in order to achieve an important goal... you understand that it is possible to achieve with humans as it is with ants... you understand about the way you would like to conduct yourself... the way in which you want to enjoy the power of the group...

I will be quiet for two minutes, during which you can experience the atmosphere of the nest and think about the insights you can gain from this place... you will be able to hear my voice in around two minutes...

After observing the ants, the host ant takes you to the exit... you leave with a good feeling... the outside light blinds you at first, though you slowly, slowly get used to it... the ant offers you the sweet potion and you sip it again... the potion enlarges you as well as the sense of your capabilities and qualities... they swell with each sip you take...

As you drink more, you fill your body with your strength as an individual and with your strength as part of a group... it is a wonderful, new feeling and it fills your whole body...

You bid farewell to the ant, grateful for what you received from it and its team, in the knowledge that you can always revisit... you can return to the ant nest at any time... to learn more from them... you go up the path and begin to make your way back... with the new awareness and the good feelings that you took on board on this magical journey to the nest...

Slowly, slowly and gradually, you begin to return to here, to this room, to your life, your body... you can move your feet a little... and your legs... move your body gently... move your head gently from side to side... take a deep breath... and another breath... slowly open your eyes and return at your pace to normal wakefulness... to full awareness... and to here and now.

7. The Ant Nest

8. *Improving Relationships With a Spouse*

Category:
Problem Solving

Who can benefit from this meditation?
People looking for a relationship and people looking to improve their relationship, as well as people who want to raise a family.

Unity

*You are invited to look beyond the
personal and the petty.
Connect to the social,
communal necessity.
The general direction will
help you to find
your personal direction.
Examine yourself: are you the
leader, or are you joining an
existing group,
Sharing your abilities?*

Allow yourself to find a comfortable position... pay attention to all the parts of your body and ensure they all feel comfortable... listen to sounds coming from outside... and the sounds in the room... to the sound of the music... let the music and my voice lead you into relaxation and rest... to lead you inside yourself and to relax... take a deep breath... and another deep breath... go back to breathing regularly... you will be able to pay attention to the rhythm of your breathing: does the air come in and out with ease?... you will notice how paying attention to your breath calms you more and more...

Now you are standing in the middle of a large field... it is a pleasant, spring day and a warm sun lights the field... the view around you is all green... being in nature relaxes you... allows you to rest... you enjoy smelling the scents of the field... you enjoy all this green... the excellent weather... a light breeze caresses your face... you sense that the brush of the breeze instills a deep calm in you...

When you look more closely you notice that you are surrounded by a wall... you look at the wall and sense that it has been there for a long time, though for some reason you had not noticed it until now... you are not sure – perhaps you saw it from time to time... the thought occurs to you that perhaps this wall is made of an invisible material, like feelings... or thoughts... allow yourself to observe the wall and understand what it is made from... you know that the wall separates the reality of your life from the way you would like it to be... with a better, more wonderful relationship...

The relationship you aspire to lies on the other side of the wall... a pleasant, empowering relationship... with lots of love in the heart and a sparkle in the eye... a relationship that will enable you to be you... to express your opinion... to express your feelings... a relationship in which you will receive and bestow warmth... love... consideration... a relationship that will allow you to grow... to develop... to celebrate life together... in the knowledge that this relationship is waiting for you beyond the wall... you decide to go over the wall in order to get there... however, something in you recoils... you are afraid... concerned...

You notice a small can in a corner near the wall... to your surprise, your name appears on it with some other writing: self-love... you approach the can and slowly, slowly open it... a beam of gentle light emerges from it and enwraps you... a light beam of love... love of yourself... you breathe it and it fills the whole of you...

You sense that now you will find a way to overcome this wall... to overcome the obstacle... you will be able to march yourself to the place you want to be in...

Allow yourself to re-imagine what the wall is made from and how you can cross it...

Is it a wall you can jump over?... or perhaps you can crush it?... maybe you can slowly cut pieces from it and diminish it?... or perhaps it can be moved gradually?... and maybe you have a special, personal way to get across the wall?...

I will be quiet for two minutes... I will allow you to find your way to get to the other side of the wall... you will hear my voice again in two minutes...

You got across the wall... you are pleased with your success... proud that you managed to cope with the difficulties... that you possessed the means you needed to do so... you find yourself outside the wall, on its other side, and you feel so good with yourself... you are happy in the knowledge that you overcame your internal obstacles and now you are completely open to love... you are ready... you know that even if new difficulties crop up you will be able to overcome them... just as you managed to cope with the difficulties and you got across the wall...

Beyond the wall and outside it, you can imagine yourself in your relationship... see how your partner looks... what his/her voice sounds like... what does his/her touch feel like... what can you do together... where can you go... what will you talk about?... (wait a minute)

Now you can sense how your heart is filled with love... radiating waves to your whole body, waves of love... of the ability to love yourself... to accept yourself... notice that when you love yourself and accept yourself, other people can love you easily... accept you as you are... to enjoy you and your love...

And with this sense of great love filling you, you can begin returning to the here and now... slowly, slowly... move your feet a little and your hands... let your body wake up gradually at your own pace... slowly open your eyes... take a deep breath... and another one... and gently return to regular wakefulness, to this room and to the here and now.

8. Improving Relationships With a Spouse

9. Baking Bread

Category:
Strengthening Resources

Who can benefit from this meditation?
People who are attempting processes of change and creativity and are too hasty to see them through.

Restraint

*Your desire to move quickly
encounters resistance.
However, things that operate
from outside
Enable you to understand
things inside yourself.
This is the time to be attentive to
your surroundings.
Be moderate in your
responses.*

Allow yourself to find a comfortable position and take a deep breath... and another breath... you will be able to notice your breathing... is it fast or slow?... does it move easily or does it encounter a difficulty in a particular place in your body?... pay attention to the flow of air from outside to the body and from the body back outside... and pay attention to how the progress of your breathing allows you to relax slowly, slowly...

We sometimes forget to breathe in the fast pace of everyday life... for you this is an opportunity to breathe more deeply, to breathe comfortably and enable you to rest... to let go... allow your breathing to take you deep into yourself... to the most basic experience of existence... to breathing... to the wonderful ability of the body to nourish itself with oxygen all the time... and you take a breath and another breath... and permit yourself greater and greater calm...

And now, imagine yourself sitting in a spacious kitchen... it has a large window through which you can see outside... it is a cold, winter day outside, though the kitchen you are in is warm and pleasant... you smell wonderful smells of food and it stirs you to bake fresh bread... just like the bread you like... whose good smell you can smell... feel its crispiness... and taste its wonderful taste...

And you begin to bake your bread – you mix flour and water in a large bowl... pay attention to the feel of the dough on your hands... to the kneading... to the gentle folding movements... the kneading movements relax you... your energy passes into the material... to the dough... feel the pleasure of the kneading... knowing that tasty, fresh bread is about to be baked... perhaps you would like to add other ingredients to the dough... salt? Yeast? Other spices?...

After you have shaped the dough as a uniform lump, you place it in the bowl and give it time to rise... it will take some time... dough needs time to rise... allow yourself to wait patiently for it to rise... feel how the waiting fills you with calm... and now you can rest...

The kitchen you are in has a special cupboard that looks like a spice cupboard... though in fact it contains powers, properties and abilities that can help you during the waiting... you will be able to take from the cupboard whatever can help you to wait calmly until the dough has risen... there are many resources in the cupboard, like: patience... stillness... calm... quiet... love... rest... security... and more... you can open it again and again and at any time choose what suits you best...

I will now be quiet for two minutes and will allow you to calmly choose all the resources you need... you will hear my voice again in two minutes...

And now, after you have chosen... you can close the door of the cupboard, knowing that you can always open it again and use the resources in it all you need to...

In the meantime the dough has risen and it is ready and amazingly airy... now you can prepare your bread... it is a special, individual bread that you can form in any way you choose... form your bread now... (wait a moment) and after you have formed it place it in an oiled baking tin and put it in the pre-heated oven at the desired temperature... and you sit and wait for the baking process...

It is important to let the dough bake in silence during the baking... without opening the oven door... without peeking inside... focus now on the processes you are undergoing in your life and feel how you often need time... time when it seems nothing is happening... though in fact a lot is happening within the silence, just like the bread is being baked inside the silence of the oven... it is getting baked slowly and gradually... and in you, too, processes are maturing slowly, exactly at the pace that suits you... because ripening occurs in its own time, only in silence... in rest... in calmness...

Hark, without your noticing how, a wonderful aroma of fresh bread fills the kitchen and the whole house... and you know exactly when your bread is ready and when it should be taken out of the oven... what great bread comes out when you have left it to rise and bake slowly in silence... remember, the changes you seek to make in your life need time... and your ability to let go a little and let them happen, easily...

You taste the bread and its tastes wonderful... the delicious, fresh bread strengthens your body and imbues you with a good feeling of vitality... and you know you can always return to the unique kitchen and bake lots of other things, if you want to... you will always have the necessary resources in the resources cupboard, and the knowledge will always accompany you that welcome changes that you initiate usually need time and patience, just like the bread in the oven...

You can begin to return to this room with the insights you have gained and other insights you picked up during the process... you can move your hands and your feet a little... move your head gently from side to side... take a deep breath... and another breath... slowly open your eyes and return at your pace to normal wakefulness... to full awareness... and to here and now.

9. Baking Bread

10. Meet Your Future Self

Category:
Future

Who can benefit from this meditation?
People who are interested in gaining insights from their future selves in order to be sure of their next step.

Conduct

How You Conduct Yourself
*Allow yourself to remember your good
values and qualities,
And how they serve your
personal growth.
Everything that happens now
depends on the way
you conduct yourself.
Everything will be in your favor,
If you operate with respect and
courtesy to yourself
and to others.*

Allow yourself to find a comfortable position... pay attention to every organ in your body and ensure that it feels comfortable... listen to sounds coming from outside... and the sounds in the room... to the sound of the music... let the music and my voice lead you into relaxation and rest... to take you inside yourself and to let go... take a deep breath... and another deep breath... breathe regularly... you will be able to pay attention to your breathing: does the air go in and out easily... you will be able to sense how paying attention to your breathing calms you more and more...

Imagine you receive a parcel in your mail box... a special parcel, wrapped in brown paper... your name and address are written on the wrapping... you are curious and want to find out – who is the parcel from and what is in it?... you are extremely surprised when you discover that your name also appears as the sender... this makes you very curious...

You go home and open the parcel... remove the rustling paper... inside the parcel you discover a disc and on it is written: "please watch me"... you play the disc and the image of an old woman/man similar to you, though a lot older, appears on the screen... he/she starts by saying that she is actually you, from the future... this disc was sent to you by you, from your future, when you are already old...

You sit down in a comfortable easy chair watching in amazement the old woman (or man) talking to you... happiness is spread over the face of your old image... you listen to her voice and something in it relaxes you... calms you... you listen to what she says... she tells you about her life, at her advanced age: what she is doing today... what happened and what is happening to members of her family... what concerns her... perhaps she can tell you how various matters you are dealing with at the moment end... maybe she can give you advice to help you cope with life more easily...

Your future image is healthy... wearing elegant clothes... living a good and enjoyable life... she tells you about her daily routine... and you feel it is possible to live a really good and satisfactory life for many years... you are proud of yourself at having achieved this...

I will now remain quiet for a minute and allow you to listen to her voice and watch her... you will hear my voice again in one minute...

It was fascinating to hear about your activities over the years and you are surprised to discover that when your future image finishes, you can ask her a lot more questions... you can ask her anything you want to know about her life... about things that happened to her... about changes she made in life... about the opportunities that came her way... how she dealt with difficulties... you have lots of questions and this is the time to ask about everything... allow yourself to ask all the questions that are important to you... (wait a moment).

When you have finished talking with the image, you remain seated in the easy chair... you are happy you had the opportunity to see yourself in old age, and you are happy about the discovery that you can age with such happiness... you feel that there is still a lot to expect in your life... a lot of good things await you... it floods you with a sense of serenity and happiness...

To your surprise, the image comes out of the television and approaches you... you can see how she walks... her figure... her smile... she hugs you... and reminds you to be kind to yourself... to take care of yourself... to spoil yourself... that things depend on you... on the way you conduct yourself... the way you build your life... her warm hug really excites you... you thank her for the powers she gave you at your meeting... she is also excited to see you... she wishes you well and returns to be inside the television...

In your heart you thank the present of the special DVD you received and you know you can always watch it again... and if you have more questions, you can always ask them... you return the DVD to the box...

You can begin to return to this room to the here and now with the insights you have gained and other insights you picked up during the process... you can move your hands and your feet a little... move your body gently... move your head gently from side to side... take a deep breath... and another breath... slowly open your eyes and return at your pace to normal wakefulness... to full awareness... and to here and now.

10. Meet Your Future Self

11. Picking the Fruits

Category:
Solving Problems

Who can benefit from this meditation?
People who want to see themselves succeeding, especially those who have experienced fear of success.

Peace

*When calmness and serenity reside deeply inside you,
You radiate it to outwards.
Your wholeness enables other people to feel whole.
Enjoy this wonderful period,
And build the future on solid foundations.*

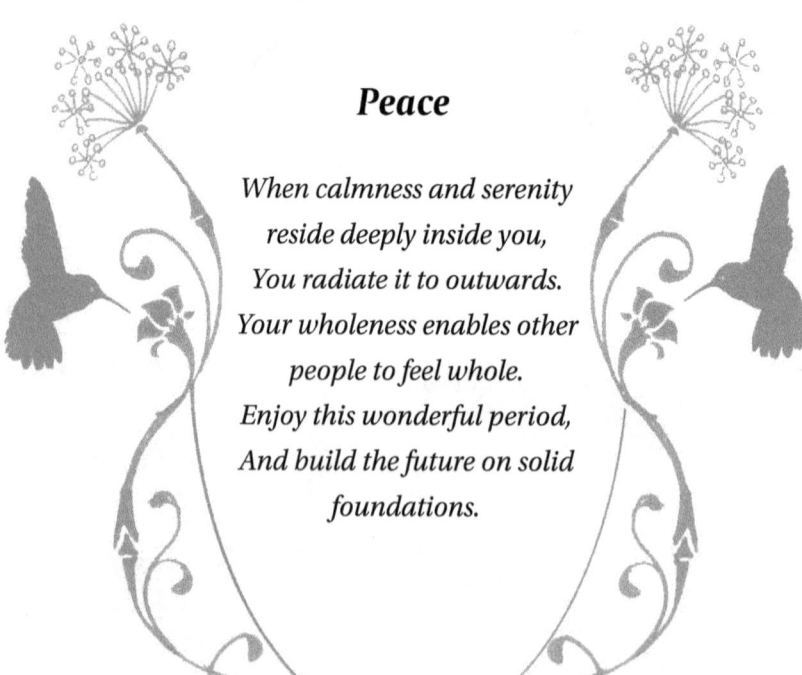

Allow yourself to find a comfortable position... for every limb in your body to feel comfortable... listen to sounds coming from outside... and the sounds in the room... to the sound of the music... let the music and my voice lead you into relaxation and rest... take a deep breath... and another deep breath... and go back to breathing normally... pay attention to the rhythm of your breathing... does the air come in and out with ease?... paying attention to your breath calms you more and more...

Imagine a pleasant spring morning... you are in a lovely country house surrounded by a garden... everything is open and possible for you... you can open the window wide and breathe in the fresh air... you can hear the twittering of birds outside the window... you feel that today you want to do something good for your growth and development... plant a new tree in the beautiful garden... a tree that will symbolize your ability to grow, to flower and produce fruit...

And you begin to move to the plant nursery to purchase a sapling of a new tree...

You go out of the door of the house and walk towards the car waiting for you outside... you intend to go to a particular nursery because you know that it is where you will find the tree that attracts you... then, you will plant it in the ground... you turn on the engine, switch on the radio and notice that something very strange is happening on the radio today... it is transmitting your thoughts, your doubts about your abilities... thoughts that prevent you from being in the place you want to be... from doing the things you want to do... yet as your thoughts are broadcast on the radio, you have the option of lowering the volume... how wonderful... allow yourself to lower the volume more and more and more... until you cannot hear those thoughts at all... or you could change the station... to a station on which good, empowering thoughts are broadcast... or a station where pleasant, relaxing songs are played... or any other station you choose... allow yourself to decide what suits you best to listen to...

You continue travelling while the radio is playing what is pleasant for you to listen to, and discover that it is difficult to see the road. The windscreen is dirty and it is hard to see the road through it... you activate the screen wash and the wipers... you notice how the view clears... you can soon see the road more easily... more clearly...

You have reached the nursery; it is just the kind of nursery you like... it has a lot of plants, saplings and trees... small, young trees... trees with lots of leaves... bigger trees... trees in plant-pots and trees in buckets... the choice is enormous and adds to your good feeling... there are also trees full of fruit at this lovely nursery... these are the trees you want... trees with leaves and fruit... that have managed to flower and produce fruit... just as you wish – to be in a place of success and prosperity... to give to the world your fruit... your abilities... your creations... knowing that you invested great effort and now is the time to pick the fruit...

I will now be quiet for about two minutes that will allow you to choose your flourishing tree and look at it... you will hear my voice again in about two minutes...

Now, after you have chosen the tree you like, you take it to the car... today you will plant it in a place you have chosen for it in your garden... you know that this tree symbolizes your success and prosperity... the fruit you produced... once you have planted it in the garden, people will be able to see it... pick its fruit... enjoy its shade... it creates in you a very good, pleasant feeling...

You return to the garden and find the special place for your tree... you dig a hole in the ground and you plant your tree of success in your garden... you see how beautiful it is... how it enriches the garden... what an intoxicating aroma it carries... you know there might be some people who do not notice it or may not like your tree... at the same time many people will like it a lot...

Just like a tree, you feel you have the courage to flower and prosper... to succeed... to set an example of your ability for others... to live at full power... to feel your full inner wholeness... to radiate your fullness and abilities to others... with love... with serenity... perhaps you believed until now that success demanded a high price... now you want to touch success and strength... and you understand that you can succeed and enjoy it... and everything will be okay... the concerns were only concerns... the wholeness you will feel inside you will extend calm and serenity to your environment...

With that pleasant feeling and with the insights you gained, you can begin to return to here, to this room... you can move your hands and feet a little... move your body gently... move your head gently from side to side... take a deep breath... and another breath... slowly open your eyes and return at your pace to normal wakefulness and to full awareness... to here and now.

11. Picking the Fruits

12. Before the Snow Melts

Category:
Solving Problems

Who can benefit from this meditation?
People who feel stuck or not sufficiently active and are interested in experiencing the growth and ripening that is occurring beneath the surface.

Stagnation

*As in the midst of winter,
There are periods when
everything freezes.
Accept this period for what it
is, and don't fight it.
Trust in your abilities
and your activities,
And wait for the snow to melt.*

Allow yourself to find a comfortable position... for every limb in your body to feel comfortable... listen to sounds coming from outside... and the sounds in the room... to the sound of the music... let the music and my voice lead you into relaxation and rest... take a deep breath... and another deep breath... and go back to breathing normally... pay attention to the rhythm of your breathing... does the air come in and out with ease?... paying attention to your breath calms you more and more...

Imagine yourself sitting in a beautiful wooden cabin located in the mountains... a hearth warms the room and spreads a relaxing warmth... the logs on the fire are colored in shades of red-orange... the fire darts about... you hear the whisper of the fire... every now and then a small spark flies and you hear the mild crack... the pleasant smell of burning wood fills the room... you are sitting opposite the window looking out... outside all is white... everything is covered with snow... piles of snow have collected all around... on the ground... on the paths... on the bushes and on the trees... there is silence outside... everything is dormant... and you feel that this dormancy gives you serenity... silence... calmness... your meditation deepens...

You look outside and the snow gives you the feeling of slowness... now you feel that in your life everything is very, very slow... too slow for you... some of the things are frozen... like the snow-covered scene... perhaps this feeling creates sadness in you... the sadness of winter...

you want to leave this slowness, you prefer more movement... where things happen faster...

Suddenly you hear the flapping of wings... a large and beautiful blue bird appears in the window opposite you... you have never seen a bird like this before... the bird approaches you... it seems to have a message in its beak... it perches on the sill of the cabin window... the very window you have been looking out of, and taps with its beak on the window... you get up and open the window for it... a mild breath of cold enters and the bird comes into the room... you close the window and discover that the bird can speak... it has an important message for you... a message you have expected for a long time...

The message intrigues you... and you are full of expectation and excitement to hear it... the beautiful, blue bird has come to reveal something important to you and you are very happy it is here... it came from far away especially for you... your whole body is filled with expectation... open to what the bird has to say...

I will be quiet for two minutes... in this time allow yourself to hear what the bird has come to say to you... listen to it... perhaps it wants to hint at how you can break out... perhaps to find a new route... to light up a path that is in your subconscious... you will hear my voice again in two minutes...

You have a remarkable feeling after hearing the bird... something has eased... maybe you had questions that you have wanted to raise for a long time... thoughts that have been causing you tension and unease... the bird has brought answers, granted you tranquility... everything is okay...

It appears that the bird has something else to say to you... it wants to remind you that the snow outside allows you to rest... enables a pause... and although there is no sign of anything happening, under the snow all is bustling and preparing for spring... the seeds, that have collected what is needed for their development for a long time, are ready and waiting to sprout... the trees are ready to bud... all have patience to wait for their moment... to wait for their flowering...

For you, too, this is an important time of preparation... even if all seems to be frozen, something is going on under the surface. Life goes on and everything is preparing for the flowering... this is the natural process and it is important to let it be... good preparation will enable the flowering in all its magnificence and beauty...

You thank the blue bird for all the insights it brought with it for you and you bid it farewell in your own way... you open the window and allow it to leave... it flies up and away... you are reminded of the dove in the story of Noah and the flood... the dove that heralds the coming of spring... you sense that spring is about to come to you, too... and you are filled with exciting, pleasant expectation of the new things it brings with it to your life...

With this comforting expectation and with the insights you have gained, you can begin to return to here, to this room... you can move your hands and feet a little... move your body gently... move your head gently from side to side... take a deep breath... and another breath... slowly open your eyes and return at your pace to normal wakefulness... to full awareness... and to here and now.

12. Before the Snow Melts

13. The Colors of Life

Category:
Strengthening Resources

Who can benefit from this meditation?
People who are interested in improving their ability to accept somebody who is different and to create a community that operates collaboratively.

Community

*This is not the time to be alone.
It is a time to initiate
and to work within your
community.
Examine yourself within your
little community –
the family: are you attentive to
its needs?
This is the time to leverage
and strengthen it.*

Allow yourself to find a comfortable position and take a deep breath... and another breath... pay attention to your breathing... is it fast or slow?... does it move easily or does it encounter a difficulty in a particular part of your body?... pay attention to the flow of air from outside to the body and from the body back outside... and notice how paying attention to your breathing enables you to relax slowly... in the fast pace of daily life we sometimes forget to breathe... for you this is an opportunity to breathe deeper and deeper, to breathe comfortably and to allow yourself to rest... to let go... let your breath take you deep inside yourself... to the experience of the most basic existence... to breathing... to the body's amazing ability to nourish itself all the time with oxygen... and you take a breath and another breath... and permit yourself more and more serenity...

Allow yourself to imagine a wave of purple color gently washing over you from the top of your head... by way of your face... the neck... chest... back... stomach... splitting to go down the arms... to the pelvis... and through the knees to reach your feet... the color purple symbolizes balance... the balance between blue and red... balance between heat and cold... the purple wave brings with it powers of balance to your life... and these powers remain in your body after the wave passes... keep the powers of balance in a place in your body that suits you... feel how the purple color enables restfulness... how the balance in your body enables you to be quiet... how things in your body and your life become balanced

Now allow yourself to imagine a green wave washing over your body... just like the previous wave... it gently passes from the top of your head to your feet... the green symbolizes growth and renewal... it symbolizes nature... it unites the coldness and wisdom of blue with the yellow of emotional warmth... the green allows you to combine your feelings and your thoughts... from where you can find your creativity... your renewal... just as nature renews itself with the coming of spring and green appears everywhere... safeguard the green powers of growth in your body... feel how the green quietly enables your growth and renewal... in the knowledge that things progress at the pace that is right for them... (wait a moment)

Now you can imagine another wave enwrapping your body... this time it is a pink wave... it enters at the top of your head and washes your whole body in pink... pink symbolizes love... your ability to love yourself and to love other people... pink also symbolizes wholeness... it strengthens your ability to accept yourself... allow yourself to feel the love and the perfection that come with it... the pink unites the red of energy with the white of simplicity... purity... innocence... let the pink remain in the special place in your body that suits it precisely... feel how the pink gives you rest... meditation... self-love, growth from day to day... until the perfection in love enwraps you...

Notice how your world is full of colors: there is purple... green... pink... and the colors that make them up... blue... red... yellow... white... each color leaves something on you... a different magical property... and now you can create a painting from all the colors, your painting... you are holding the paintbrush and you can simply take a color and another color and play with them on the paper to your heart's desire... everybody can paint a picture like this... even somebody who does not normally draw or paint... in this way you paint your special picture... allow yourself to mix the colors and create a painting... notice how all the colors blend into a wonderful harmony...

Allow yourself to enjoy your world enriched by color... just like a rainbow or a beautiful, colorful painting... just as each color brings its uniqueness to the painting, so each person in your life brings his/her uniqueness – a community of people can paint a painting together and create collaboration from the difference and the variety of each person... a whole is created that is greater than each of the individuals in it... just as our world is full of color... which is how you feel in your family... both close and extended... and just as the difference in the colors creates a unique colorful texture, so your life in a community... is filled with color...

Sometimes it is difficult to accept colors that are not yours... at the same time, when you remember how these colors enrich your life, you are thankful for them and enjoy them...

You slowly, slowly begin to return with this celebration of color to this room... to the colors in it... you separate from the colors that existed somewhere out there, on your journey... slowly, slowly you can begin to return to normal wakefulness... to normal awareness... you can move your hands and feet a little... open your eyes at your own pace... and return to here and now.

13. The Colors of Life

14. Gratitude

Category:
Past

Who can benefit from this meditation?
People who are grateful for the abundance they have and wish to summon additional abundance into their lives.

Many assets

*You are blessed with great success
and abundance!
Maintain your modesty and
your compassion,
And advance matters
for the general good.
In this way you will create
a stance of authority for yourself,
And you will serve as an
example for others.*

Allow yourself to find a comfortable position… for every limb in your body to feel comfortable… listen to sounds coming from outside… and the sounds in the room… to the sound of the music… let the music and my voice lead you into relaxation and rest… take a deep breath… and another deep breath… and go back to breathing normally… pay attention to the rhythm of your breathing… does the air come in and out with ease?… paying attention to your breath calms you more and more…

Imagine yourself sitting next to a beautiful, round fishpond, in which goldfish and other fish of different colors are swimming… leaves of different sizes are floating on the surface of the water… in different shades of green… and two pink lotus flowers blossom calmly on the waters of the pond…

You can hear the whisper of the wind around you and the twittering of the birds… it is a pleasant spring day… and you are sitting on a large rock next to the pond and enjoying the sun's warming rays… perfect weather… you can feel the brush of the breeze caressing your face and body… you feel more and more comfortable… a wave of relaxation and calmness moves from the top of your head… through your face… neck… chest… enwraps your hands… and via the stomach… the pelvis… to your feet and washes over your whole body…

You calmly observe the goldfish swimming at their leisure, and you think about all the things in your life for which you are grateful…

for the wonderful nature around you and everything it generates... for lovely days of pleasant sunshine... or perhaps for rainy days that bring blessings... each of us likes different weather... and different shades of nature... take a breath and thank nature... for all the things it brings with it for you...

And the wave of calmness crosses you again... from the top of your head to your feet... and through it you are grateful for all the parts of your body... that work well for you... that enable you to be light-footed... that enable you to move freely... allow yourself to thank your body for every day you feel good... for every healthy part of your body... and send a healing calmness and love to the parts that ache... (wait a moment)

You look compassionately at the pink flowers and the green leaves around you... they look like a family to you... and you remember other things that you can be grateful for now... for the close and dear members of your family... perhaps for your good friends who stand with you in both difficult and happy times... it is likely that you remember various events in your life, good things that happened to you in the past...

The calmness fills you and you are grateful for yourself, too... for all the good things you do... for your desire to develop and learn... for your ability to advance and to advance others... for permitting yourself this pause... remind yourself of all the nice things you do for yourself and for others and thank yourself for doing so... be grateful for the positive thoughts in your head... be grateful for the moments of happiness... of love... of acceptance... you can breathe your gratitude in deeply and place it right inside your body...

Perhaps you are grateful for something your learned... for progress of change in your life... or for an exceptional achievement?...

I will now be quiet for two minutes, in which you can be grateful for all the good things life has brought you... in another two minutes you will hear my voice again...

Allow yourself to be grateful also for the difficult things that life throws up... in the knowledge that you can learn from everything... to grow... to develop and advance... even when it seems hard... your heart is full of gratitude and you feel that the more you remember the good things in your life and the more you are grateful for them, the more good things will happen in your life... from what there is we create more for ourselves... greater abundance... take a deep breath and fill yourself with this feeling...

Every day you can remember and be more and more grateful for the good things in your life... small and big... every day new, good things will enter your life... more and more... and knowing this you can begin to return from the fishpond to here and to now... to your life, your body... you can move your hands and feet a little... move your body gently... move your head gently from side to side... take a deep breath... and another breath... slowly open your eyes and return at your pace to normal wakefulness... to full awareness... and to here and now.

14. Gratitude

15. Hills of Moderation

Category:
Solving Problems

Who can benefit from this meditation?
People who want to deal calmly with their surroundings.

Humility

*In times of moderation,
nothing is extreme.
Match yourself to this period:
Moderate your answers and
your fixed opinions.
Find a delicate balance.
Humility will help you along
your way.*

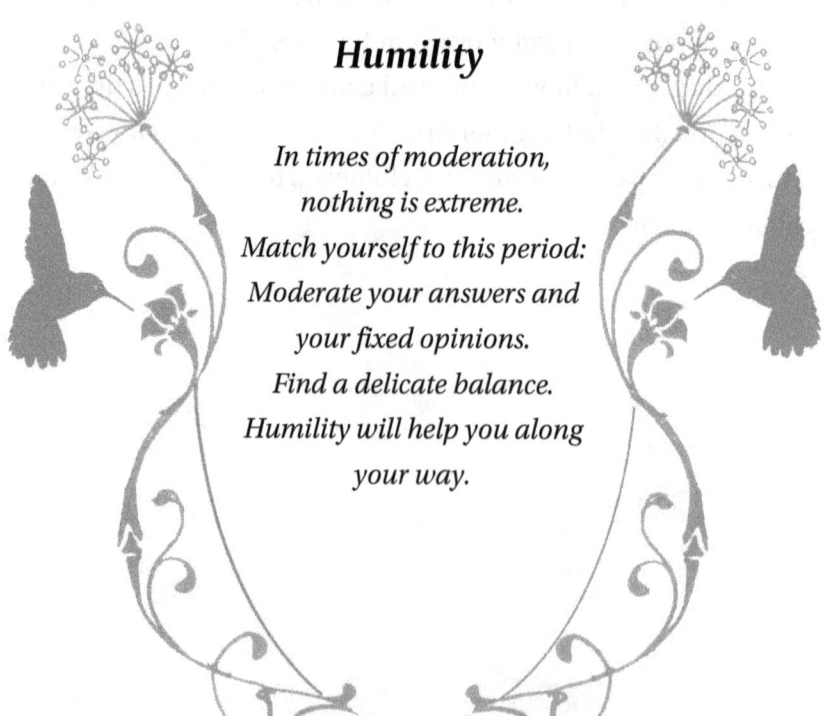

Allow yourself to close your eyes and to find a comfortable position for your body... take a deep breath and permit yourself to rest... let your body rest from all the day's activity... every part of your body can relax and slowly, slowly enter an atmosphere of calm and tranquility... it is likely that lots of thoughts are going through your mind... let the thoughts move on... move beyond you and allow your head to empty and to slowly, slowly fill with pleasant calmness...

You are in a mountainous area, high... you raise your gaze and look at the sky... from where you are you can see various shapes of clouds... some are shiny, white sheep clouds... some are soft feather clouds... around you the mountains are jagged... very high... you look at the mountains and sense their strength... at the same time, their jagged, sharp shape causes you to feel a little uncomfortable...

It is a pleasant, warm day... the sun's rays break through the clouds and pleasantly caress your body... a light breeze is blowing... you can hear its murmur... the aroma of familiar wild flowers reaches your nose... you are standing on a ridge at the foot of a very high mountain and are looking at it... perhaps you are reminded how small a person is next to a massive mountain like this... you are in awe of nature... of the ability of nature to create such high mountains next to deep valleys... the mountains transmit a powerful silence... a sense of humility fills you...

You are impressed by the power of nature and by the wonderful connection between size and strength and calmness and tranquility... you ponder the idea that in your life there are also periods of extremism... periods in which the mountains seems very high... and the valleys very steep... and then, after conquering the high peaks, there are sometimes plunges... at these times you feel that your feelings are very volatile... perhaps you feel the need to express anger... or affront... disappointment... or sadness... everything is very unsettled... and perhaps, like the jagged mountains, your opinions are sometimes very fixed and clear to you... periods of clarity...

And you start walking in the direction of the mountain... it is very, very big... slightly threatening... though it has something that attracts you... the mountain invites you to go inside it... and as you approach it you notice a small door... a door hewn in the rock that invites you to go inside, actually inside the mountain... you open the door... it is dark inside the mountain... it takes a few minutes for your eyes to get used to the darkness... at the same time, you notice a tiny, darting light approaching you from the path in the belly of the mountain...

The light comes closer... and closer... and you see an old Chinese man walking towards you and he reaches you... he has an oil lamp in his hand... he gives a little nod and with a wave of his hand invites you to follow him into the mountain... you follow him and you can hear the sound of his steps... there is a strong echo inside the mountain and your steps are also heard... it is a very long corridor... and you wonder, what is hiding in the heart of the mountain?...

You reach a small nook and the old man invites you to sit on a small chair... a special scent arises from a candle burning there... the old man sits down opposite you and offers you a small wooden box with "humility" written on it in English and Chinese... you open the box and see a sheet of paper taken from the I Ching, on which is written: "humility is a hidden quality, like a small box in the heart of a mountain"... you are thrilled by the occasion and the fact that you have reached the heart of the mountain, and you continue to read what is on the page... "humility is the goal of a person walking the good path... although it is unseen, it shines from afar... nature acts moderately... subtracts from what is full and fills what is empty... which is the way a person acts with moderation... with flexibility"...

You look at the old Chinese man affably and chose to enjoy the quiet and the calm of the silence... the old Chinese man invites you to get up from the chair and leads you further... you go further into the depths of the mountain... while you are walking in the belly of the mountain you are pondering the things that were written in the box... you think about your wish that things were more relaxed... calmer... to grant more harmony to your life... that the box in the heart of the mountain will remain with you and lead to insights when you want them... you continue to follow the old man and notice that you are in fact crossing the mountain from inside... a tiny light shines from afar, and you know that soon you will emerge on the other side of the mountain... you think it will be interesting to discover what there is on the other side...

You reach the exit and go out... sunlight greets you, and the old Chinese man bids you farewell and returns inside the mountain... you thank him and turn to look around... your eyes slowly get accustomed to the light outside... you are surprised to discover how much the view has changed on the other side of the mountain: instead of sharp, high mountains there are low round hills... at the side of which are lovely little valleys... all covered with fresh grass, and rivers flow between the hills... the view is beautiful and now much more moderate... pleasant... likeable... here it is easier to climb the hills and go down into the valleys... it is possible to quench your thirst from the streams and to be filled with tranquility and harmony... you drink from one of the small streams and recline at the foot of the hill...

And with this sense of moderation and tranquility, slowly, slowly and gradually you begin to return to here, to this room, to your life, to your body... you can move your hands and feet a little... move your body gently... move your head gently from side to side... take a deep breath... and another breath... slowly open your eyes and return at your pace to normal wakefulness... to full awareness... and to here and now.

15. Hills of Moderation

16. Pamper Yourself Day

Category:
Strengthening Resources

Who can benefit from this meditation?
People who need a break and to be pampered a bit.

Enthusiasm

Everything is now in harmony.
You can develop
by listening to yourself,
And by believing
in your own abilities.
Things work out for you,
Thanks to the wonderful match
between you and the universe.

Allow yourself to find a comfortable position... for every limb in your body to feel comfortable... close your eyes and focus on your head... you will feel how it feels inside... relax your head and notice how pleasant it is to pay calm attention to the head... and now you can move around your whole body with this calm attention... slowly, slowly and gently... feel how much it relaxes you... perhaps you can hear the sounds coming from outside... and the sounds in the room... these sounds and the sound of the music playing help you to focus your attention on all the parts of your body... down to your feet... and when your attention reaches your feet, the calm and serenity in you increases...

Imagine yourself waking up from a good night's sleep in a lovely house you are in for a vacation... slowly, slowly you get up from the bed... go to the window, open the shutters and look outside; you discover that after a very long winter... which was cold... winds blew... there were very few leaves on the trees... a lot of rain fell... after a long period of winter, finally spring has arrived...

The warm sun embraces the trees and its rays color everything in a soft light... the trees appear to have been washed... they are ready for spring... the sun has sprouted little leaves on their branches, new and fresh... new flower buds are popping up everywhere... some of them reveal the future color of the flowers: pink... red... purple... the colors blend in with the green around and there are still small drops of dew hanging on the trees...

Birds are perched on the branches of the trees, chirping... to your ears the chirping sounds like pleasant, relaxing music... a feeling of happiness fills your heart... you feel enthusiasm... happiness... something has changed... you feel as if you have also been submerged in a prolonged winter... now your spring has arrived... everything is starting to bloom and flower...

And you decide to celebrate this wonderful spring. You get dressed and get ready to go out... and when you go outside to the garden, you discover that a lavish breakfast awaits you there... you sit at the table... you partake of food made exactly how you like it... breathe the fresh, invigorating air... smell the pleasant aromas of the flowering... how good it is to begin the morning like this...

During the tasty breakfast, you feel you fancy doing something different today... something you have wanted to do for a long time... something special for yourself... a real pampering... today you really want to pamper yourself... to feel as if you are also a flower that has waited the whole winter and is now beginning to flower... and it needs a little water... and a little sunshine... and a bit of fertilizer in order to open fully...

You also need a little pampering so you can flower... and today you decide that it is a great time to pamper yourself... you realize how essential it is for you to do something only for yourself... it could be a massage... or a warm bath... or a special fun trip you have always wanted to make... or read a good book... or see a good movie... anything you love doing and will do you good...

I will now be quiet for two minutes, in which you can do something to pamper yourself... allow yourself to experience it and to enjoy yourself... you will hear my voice again in two minutes...

Your pampering is still going on... you are getting ready to end it today... it was so lovely to pamper yourself... you feel you are still in a great mood... you reenter the house in a relaxed way and listen to the music that you like most... perhaps you want to invite friends to spend the rest of the day with you... or maybe you will just want to be alone... in your own quiet... listen to the music that fills the space of the house, spreading pleasant sounds everywhere... filling your heart...

You feel it to be a wonderful day... full of pampering and pleasure... and you believe that you will be able to create other days like this for yourself... or moments like this... you know that in order to develop and grow you have to listen to yourself... pamper yourself... invest in yourself... in order to create and do; it is worth also having fun... and life can offer us all sorts of enjoyment, small and big... if we make a point of remembering now and again... if we are able to invest a little in ourselves...

You know that as time passes you will be able to invest in yourself more and more... it fills you with happiness and joy like you experienced now... and with this feeling you begin to return to here, to this room... you can move your hands and feet a little... move your body gently... move your head gently from side to side... take a deep breath... and another breath... slowly open your eyes and return at your pace to normal wakefulness... to full awareness... and to here and now.

16. Pamper Yourself Day

17. Simple Flow

Category:
Finding direction

Who can benefit from this meditation?
People who are want to loosen control and to go with the flow, to be like water...

Adaptation

At the moment you have to behave,
By adapting to what is happening around you.
If you find it difficult to adapt, work on self-change.
Good adaptation will enable you to find tranquility,
And in that way you will be able to succeed in what you do.

Allow yourself to find a comfortable position... grant yourself the possibility to rest... your body works hard and exerts itself during the whole day and this is an opportunity to let go a little... and when you are comfortable on the mattress or on a chair, you will feel how all the places in your body where tension has built up will slowly, slowly loosen up and relax... it is a pleasant feeling of release... allow yourself to take a deep breath and another breath and to let the air flow in your body... the air flows in the open areas and sometimes it struggles to flow where there are blockages... direct awareness to these areas and enable them to open up... take another breath... and another one... feel how the air brings with it a tranquility and calmness into your body, to every corner... and you feel more connected to the quiet inside you...

Now imagine yourself standing next to a river on a bright summer day... the river is clear, and the water seems pure and good... the river flows slowly down a moderate slope, and something inside you calls you to get into it... to have a pleasant swim in the river... something about this river attracts you... without thinking too much you dip your feet into the water... and slowly your whole body goes in... the river is large and wide... its water is blue-green... clear, clear... you can hear the trickle of the water... sense its cold touch... smell its pleasant smell... this is a special river... it enables you to move easily with the flow of the water in it... to free yourself from control and simply loosen up in its cold, pleasant water...

You float on the surface of the water and you can feel how the water is directing your body... and you are going with it on a wonderful journey... perhaps it is slightly hard for you initially with the water directing you, deciding for you on the direction to go... or the pace... though very quickly you understand that this is a special journey on which you permit yourself to relax... to be led by the water... the water floats you along gently... calmly... pleasantly... and you are swept away with it... trouble free... and as it continues to take you, you sense how its touch caresses and lets you relax even more... and more... and more... to rest... simply drifting and floating...

The river continues to take you... you see the vegetation around you, on the river bank and beyond it... the scene is green and well-shaded... in some places the river becomes narrow and you can hardly get through... at times it is very wide... and you have lots of room... at times rocks appear in the river and the water takes you carefully to the side of them and protects you from them... here and there little fish nibble at your feet... you do nothing except let the water take you along... you know it is taking care of you... and you let it take you through all the states of the river...

The water enables you to try out your ability to allow processes to occur by themselves... simply to let things be... you are happy to discover that even when you let go, everything is alright... things happen as they are supposed to... quietly... and calmly... you can let things happen by themselves... and you can free yourself from having to manage them... you think about the tiredness that has built up in your body from trying to control things and manage them... and now the water is allowing you a good rest... you dissolve the tiredness... you have a sense of release... and flow... you can flow with the water... as with many other things in life... you can let the current take you... you get used to the new feeling... a feeling of rest... of belief...

The water returns you to the river bank... a large towel awaits you... you get out of the water, towel off, the sun's rays warm you and dry you... there are clean clothes ready for you on the fresh grass and you put them on... you detect that something has changed in your movement: you are lighter... as if you are free of what you have been carrying with you for a long time... you move more freely and more easily and with freedom... and pleasant calmness continues to accompany you...

A beautiful butterfly lands on your hand... you look at it... it is colorful and spectacular... and it is standing calmly on your hand... you can actually feel the fluttering of its wings... this butterfly symbolizes your ability to change... your ability to be light and free just like it... it stays on your hand for a few more seconds and then flies off... you are light and relaxed and can go on your way...

With this wonderful, light feeling you begin to return to here, to this room... you can move your hands and feet a little... take a deep breath... gently open your eyes... and slowly you return... at your own pace to normal wakefulness... and to here and now.

17. Simple Flow

18. The Frogs' Song

Category:
Solving Problems

Who can benefit from this meditation?
People who feel that an aspect of their life has been neglected and they want to do something about it.

Repair

*At the moment something
is being neglected,
And hard work is needed to
repair it and to succeed.
Take three days to think about
it before you begin.
Find a way of repairing what
was broken,
And perform a thorough repair.
Hard, thorough work will
result in great success.*

Let yourself find a comfortable position... you will be able to feel your body on the chair or on the mattress... you are at rest and you slowly, slowly begin to experience a sense of comfort... it is a time of rest for you... for your body... it is a time that permits your head to free itself a little from thoughts and loosen up... you will be able to hear voices from outside... allow yourself to focus on my voice... feel how calmness fills you... and you feel more and more relaxed from minute to minute...

Imagine yourself on a pleasant autumn day... above the sky is cloudy... a pleasant breeze is blowing... you are sitting next to an old stone house... it seems it was built a long time ago... just below the house there is a small pond... it looks beautiful and alluring, at the same time, when you approach it, you notice that the water in the pond is filthy... it is dirty and full of slime... it saddens you... you would like the water to be clear and clean... then flowers would be able to grow on it... and fish could swim in it...

Sometimes it seems that things are standing still in your life... like murky water... something that you want to happen is not happening... something is stuck, stagnant... simplicity is missing... clarity is missing... purity is missing...

Something inside you tells you that you have the ability to change the water in the pond... to change your life... to make things right and better for you... and you begin to think how you can clean the pond... what can you do to create clarity and purity?

You sit on a stone next to the pond and wonder where to start... what you can do to correct what is damaged... so that things turn out differently... you contemplate this... you realize that you have seen this pond in the past... you remember it... then it was clear and pure... you want to feel like you used to... at a time when the pond was clear... bright... when looking at the water was accompanied by happiness, by pleasure...

You notice an old man approaching and stopping next to you... he has a feathered crown on his head and he looks like a Red Indian chief... his movements are heavy and deliberate... you look at his face and can see that he is a very wise old man... he sits down next to you and tells you a story... he has a very pleasant voice and you are surprised that he is talking in your language... he tells you that the Indians believe that frogs carry purification energy... the croaking of frogs brings rain... the rain purifies the ground, the people and the water sources...

You listen to what the wise Indian has to say and are filled with thoughts... he gets up to go and gives you a box with a perforated lid... you open it and find in it seven big frogs... you release the frogs on the banks of the pond... they immediately jump in and disappear under the water... after a few minutes they get out of the water and begin to croak... their croaking sounds pleasing, like a lovely song... you listen to the song and realize that they are singing a song for rain...

Slowly, slowly, and gradually rain begins to fall... you enter the old stone house and leave the door open... through the door you can see the drops of rain bouncing on the ground... you can hear the sound of the rain and the sound of the frogs that can still be heard between the drops... you can smell the wonderful smell of the rain... the smell of the ground embracing it...

Everything is washed and revitalized... the ground is soaked, as is the pond... the drops prance on the surface of the pond... the rain continues to fall... sometimes it is heavier and pounds the earth, and sometimes soft drops fall gently from the sky... until it stops...

You go out of the house and look around you... the pond is now completely different... the water is pure and clear... it is wonderful to see how the rain cleaned it... and the sky is reflected in it... you feel the same way about your life... you are able to bring about change... perhaps you can be assisted by people around you to repair the things that are not right for you... and you can also use your inner resources to do this... you can be helped by your abilities... by your good qualities...

The sun's rays emerge from between the clouds and create lines of light on the pond and on you... the line of light on you changes with the movement of the clouds and gives you the sense of the purity in the change... a colorful rainbow appears in the sky... you feel great joy at seeing the rainbow... you feel that the rainbow offers you hope... enables you to continue from here in a good and correct direction for you...

And with this wonderful feeling you begin to return to here... to this room... to the reality of your life... you take with you the good feeling that everything can be changed... and that in time things can change... you have the power to do so... and your power will gain strength as time goes on...

With this feeling you slowly, slowly and gently begin to return to normal wakefulness and normal reality... you can move your hands and feet a little... take a deep breath... slowly open your eyes... and return here and now.

18. The Frogs' Song

19. An Ancient Chinese Saying

Category:
Strengthening Resources

Who can benefit from this meditation?
People who need encouragement
and a message of progress and success.

Progress

*Spring lets you begin to grow,
And progress along
the right road for you.
You can develop towards
self-realization.
All the conditions
for spiritual growth,
Are now at your disposal.*

Allow yourself to find a comfortable position... close your eyes and let yourself focus your attention on your head... to sense how it feels inside... relax your head... notice how pleasant it is to pay relaxed attention to your head... now you can travel all around your body with this relaxed attention... slowly, slowly and gently... feel how it relaxes... you hear sounds from outside or inside the room... these sound and the sound of the music playing help you to focus your attention on all parts of your body... down to your feet... and when your attention reaches your feet, you are already very, very relaxed and calm...

Imagine yourself at the entrance of an ancient house... the house is built in an ancient style, and something about it really attracts you to enter it... the door is open and inviting and you sense you are wanted inside it... because it is alright to enter this house and look at it... when you enter you see the large rooms, the old furniture... you are very curious to know what is in this house... who lives in it... you touch the furniture and go round the rooms, and then you see steps leading to the basement...

You start going down... there are more steps than you thought and they are a little dark... however, a little light is enough for you to go down safely... you feel calm and relaxed... and as you go further down the steps, your calmness increases... something in you senses that you will find something very interesting in the basement of the house... that something is waiting there for you...

You continue to descend... you adapt your eyes more and more to the darkness and feel secure and protected... until you reach a large basement... you look around you and see lots of cartons, and you are yearning to know what is concealed inside them... you open one of the cartons and discover that it is full of ancient books... the books arouse your curiosity, you take one of the books in your hand and feel it... smell it's smell... the smell of an archaic book...

When your eyes have got accustomed to the dimness you recognize what is written on the cover of the book: "The I Ching"... you read on the front pages that it is a book of predictions... that the Chinese used it to predict what would happen in the future... then you see a page with your name written on it... and it goes on, "please open me on one of the pages and read what is written... it is a message for you... and it will symbolize the near future for you"...

You again read what is written... because it is a little difficult to believe that your name appears in such an ancient book... and then you close the book and open it again randomly... on the page that opens is written: "Hexagram 19: Progress – great success. A very promising situation that allows you to advance things... to be active... lots of luck will shine on you"...

You are excited by the message you received from the I Ching... the message suits you now... and you happily repeat the words... great success... luck will shine on you... ability to progress... you feel how these words encourage you... create a sense of ability in you... of capability... and you imagine yourself progressing... succeeding... an expression of happiness on your face... and fortune favors you... you are so happy to see yourself like this...

You look again at the page of the book and you notice that your name is written in small letters at the bottom of the page... and there is a little note there on which is written: "write a wish"... you open the note and begin to write...

I will now be quiet for one minute to allow you to write your wish... you will hear my voice again in one minute...

And when you have written down your wish, you realize you have been in the basement for a long time... the time has come to go back up again... you conceal the note between the pages of the book and return the book to the carton... you want to look at more books... you are not in a hurry... something tells you that you can always return to the house and the basement and you will have the opportunity to peruse all the books the next time...

You begin to ascend the stairs... more and more... feeling you have had a surprising, unexpected and very interesting visit to the basement... and now... full of the special experience you underwent, you return to the ancient house... go out of the door and slowly begin to return to here, to this room... the sense of progress, success and good fortune accompany you as you slowly return to normal awareness... when you open your eyes you are able to remember your picture and the message you received... these are all yours...

And with these delightful presents... you slowly and gently begin to return to normal wakefulness and to normal reality... you can move your hands and feet... take a deep, filling breath, slowly open your eyes... and return to here and now.

19. An Ancient Chinese Saying

20. Journey with the Wind

Category:
Finding direction

Who can benefit from this meditation?
People who need a moment of contemplation in order to look at their life differently.

Contemplation

*In your magical way,
You are invited to devote some time
to calm reflection.
When you look deeply
at the situation,
You will discover important
insights regarding your path.
You will also be able
to direct yourself,
In anticipation of what
lies ahead.
Reflection increases
your strength.*

Allow yourself to find a comfortable position... you will be able to feel your body on the chair or on the mattress... loosen the muscles a little... and slowly begin to get the feeling of comfort... this is a time of rest for you... for the body... a time that allows the head to get rid of the thoughts and to loosen up... let your thoughts dissolve like bright clouds in the sky that move with the wind, dissolve and disappear... you will be able to hear voices from outside and the music playing here in the room... allow yourself to focus on my voice... and feel how you become more and more comfortable from minute to minute...

Imagine yourself standing on a small hill... there are other hills surrounding you, some are higher, some lower; the hills are all shades of green... the plants around move in the wind... the aroma of the plants reaches your nose... you look at the hills and feel the brush of the breeze on your face... you hear its soft whisper... the wind is trying to tell you something... listen well to the voice of the wind... the wind invites you to accompany it on a magical journey across the surface of the earth...

You feel you are drawn to the wind and you begin to fly with it... flying over the land is pleasant for you... the fluctuations of the wind bring up your old memories of fluctuations... perhaps from your infancy... perhaps from your mother's tummy... you sense how the rolling and rocking calms you more and more... they are so pleasant... they make you feel protected... you know that this flight is safely taking you on a special journey...

You are flying and you can see the view around you... the green hills change into other views... green or rocky mountains... yellowed plains... brown ploughed fields... and you can even see the sea from afar... you feel your spirits are high as you look at the ground spread out below you in all its glory... you are enjoying the flight... and reflect...

Reflection allows you to remember your ability simply to be... simply to reflect on your life... and when you first reflect and only afterwards act, things are done in a better way... in a way that allows you to understand the situation... and to formulate your mode of operating slowly and gradually...

The Chinese believe that people who know how to reflect silently can predict situations and know how to prepare for what lies ahead... you understand that the wind has taken you on a journey in order to teach you its way... the way of reflection... the wind gently changes the view... slowly, slowly... gradually... and in this way you can also reflect on and understand what you would like to leave as it is and what you would like to change... what serves you in your life and what things you can dispense with... (wait a moment).

You continue to glide along on the wings of the good wind... and look at the changes taking place below you... the sun begins to set... and after a day, rises again... the changing seasons in the places you visit... you move between spring, summer, autumn and winter... you look around you and are amazed by nature working and allowing things to happen in their own time and at their own pace...

Now the wind slows down and descends, and you see that you have returned to the green hill from which you set out on the journey... you thank the wind for enabling you to see the world from its viewpoint... the wind invites you to join it whenever you want and hopes that with time you can develop your ability to reflect... the ability to predict... and continues on its endless flight...

And with this good feeling, you collect the insights the wind granted you and slowly begin to return to here, to this room... to your life on earth... you return to normal reality... at your own pace, you move your hands and feet a little... slowly and gently you open your eyes... and return to here and now.

20. Journey with the Wind

21. The Display Window

Category:
Future

Who can benefit from this meditation?
People who are interested in changing and to see the change in their life.

Basic change

*Like the air you breathe,
You need a fundamental change
in your life.
You cannot avoid changing
what no longer serves you.
You will need to work on
yourself in order to know,
What will enable you to develop
in directions that are good
for you,
And what holds you back.*

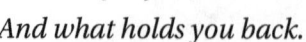

Allow yourself to find a comfortable position... you will be able to feel your body on the chair or on the mattress... and slowly begin to get the feeling of comfort... this is a time of rest for you... for the body... a time that allows the head to get rid of the thoughts and to loosen up... you will be able to hear voices from outside and the music playing here in the room... allow yourself to focus on my voice... and feel how calmness fills you... and feel how you become more and more comfortable from minute to minute...

And now imagine yourself walking along a main street in a city... you look at the display windows of the stores... cars pass you on the street you are on... you can hear the sound of the engines... some buses also pass by... some of them stop at the stop near you and people get off and on... you can hear the peoples' voices... and smell the smell of the busy city...

You continue walking and looking... the city is noisy and full of life... and the more the city bustles, so you are less and less attentive to the loud noises... the calmness inside you increases... you continue walking slowly, and serenity fills you... you pass various stores... you stop for a moment when something attracts your attention... and then you move on...

After a while your reach an electrical goods store... in the store's display window two television screens are displayed and they are both showing the same picture... you stop to watch and are surprised to see that you appear on the television screens... you look to the side to see if anybody else has noticed this... though only you alone are standing at the display window...

An old salesman comes out to you from the store... he explains that these are very special television screens... and people who are interested can see their future in them... he says that if you look carefully you will be able to see your future, like it will be once you have dealt with what is troubling you at the moment... there are two screens, therefore you will be able to see two future pictures... in two different spheres of life...

You stand and look... the picture of you as you are today appears on the screens... you begin to get very excited when you notice that something is starting to change... you have a rare opportunity to see yourself as you would like to look... one of the screens is showing a different, new picture, of your future... and the other screen also begins to change...

I will now be quiet for two minutes and allow you to look at the pictures on the television screens... you will be able to create desirable future pictures of yourself... perhaps the pictures with be a serial story... perhaps each of them will come from a different aspect of life... you will hear my voice again in two minutes.

What excitement... the pictures are there in front of you on the television screens and the old salesman goes into the store for a moment... he comes out with the pictures printed and offers them to you... you thank him very much and he invites you to look at the television screens whenever you want to... perhaps it will be when you have already achieved your goals and you want to set new goals... or perhaps when you want to be reminded of the pictures you saw today...

You cast another glance at the new pictures of you on the screens and leave the man... you continue striding along the streets of the busy city... calmly, slowly and quietly... and slowly you begin to return to here, to this room, to your body, to this special day... you can lock the new pictures into your heart and you can let them lead you further... and now you can begin to return... you can move your hands and feet a little... and at your own pace slowly open your eyes... and return to here and now.

21. The Display Window

22. The Hot Air Balloon

Category:
Strengthening Resources

Who can benefit from this meditation?
People who are interested in travelling to places they have dreamed of getting to.

A moment of grace

*This is a unique moment,
more valuable than gold,
A wonderful moment of pleasure.
What is happening at present
is not connected to reality.
It passes.
Let yourself enjoy a period full
of inspiration and creativity.
Capture the magical moment.
It is here and it is yours,
Though don't draw
conclusions from it about
the future.*

Let yourself find a comfortable position... you can feel your body on the chair or on the mattress... you are resting and slowly begin to experience a sense of ease... it is a time of rest for you... for your body... it is a time to allow your head to let go a little of the thoughts and to loosen up... you can hear voices from outside... allow yourself to focus on my voice... and feel how calmness fills you... and you feel more and more comfortable from moment to moment...

Imagine yourself standing in a wide, green field... decorated by tiny flowers... you look at the magnificent view in front of you... enjoying the beauty and the delicate aroma of the flowers... you can feel the wind blowing and relaxing you... all around is calm and serene...

A giant hot air balloon appears in the field... it is colorful and beautiful... it has a large basket... an old man gets out of the basket and invites you to get on board...

You get into the large basket and feel its special texture... there are soft, comfortable cushions in it... the old man invites you to sit down... he steers the balloon that slowly gains height...

As the balloon rises, so a pleasant calmness fills your body... you hear the pleasant sound of the wind and feel it on your skin... you feel that soon you will be able to touch the clouds... the balloon rises and the scenery changes... with every additional rise you see more and more views spread out below you... and a wider and fuller picture of the world faces you...

The balloon slowly approaches the clouds... it reaches the first cloud and goes into it... you are covered by the light touch of cotton wool... the touch is soft and pleasant... inside the cloud everything you see is blurred and you float among the mists... when you leave the cloud a wonderful scene is spread out below you... from where you can see a great distance... it is a unique view... a view exactly as you like it... you feel lucky for having had such a wonderful journey in a magical hot air balloon, and in perfect weather...

The old man steers the balloon that continues to float in the sky... he makes a circuit so you can see scenery in more and more places... you can choose a place you have always dreamed about visiting and ask the balloon to take you there... you can reach distant lands you dreamed of visiting...

I will now be quiet for two minutes to allow you to visit all the places you want to... to every vista you have been to and perhaps to those you have dreamed of... you will hear my voice again in about two minutes...

You are happy to have been given the opportunity to visit beautiful places you have always dreamed of going to... you feel pleasant and full... a feeling of perfection... the balloon begins to descend... it is time to begin to return home... the old man steers the balloon to face your home and slowly and gradually lowers it... you enjoy the wind blowing on your face... you enjoy the touch of the cloud you pass through on your way back...

And you notice that on the ground below you a sentence has been written just for you, in big letters... it is a message you can take with you from your trip in the hot air balloon... it's a message that can stay with you... look down and notice the message... perhaps you can also hear it echoing in your ears...

(wait a moment)

With this message, and with the feeling of spiritual elevation from the heavenly journey, the balloon gets lower and lower... finally landing on the ground... and you descend from it with the help of the old man... he bids you farewell and invites you to have other trips in the hot air balloon whenever you wish... with a smile you thank him and begin to slowly return to here, to this room... to your body resting on the mattress... to this special day... lock the new pictures and the message you received into your heart and let them accompany you as you move forward...

And with this wonderful feeling you slowly return... allow yourself to move your hands a little... and to move your feet... gently open your eyes, and at your own pace return to here and now.

22. The Hot Air Balloon

23. The Puzzle of My Life

Category:
Future

Who can benefit from this meditation?
People who feel that their life is coming apart and are interested to create a complete picture of reality.

Disintegration

*It is a time of difficulties
and delays.
Therefore you can do
nothing besides
strengthening yourself,
And taking care of your health
till the period ends.
Then you can re-build,
and success will come.*

Let yourself find a comfortable position... a pleasant position for you... you can feel your body on the chair or on the mattress... you are resting and slowly begin to experience a sense of ease... it is a time of rest for you... for your body... it is a time to allow your head to let go a little of the thoughts and to loosen up... slowly and gradually your thoughts dissolve like light clouds that scatter in the wind on a summer day... you can hear voices from outside... allow yourself to focus on my voice... and you feel more and more comfortable from moment to moment...

Imagine yourself sitting in a spacious, bright house... a large, beautiful house... you are sitting in one of the rooms... there is a table next to you on which pieces of a puzzle are haphazardly dispersed... you look at it and see lots of pieces spread around... in various different colors... you can feel them... a pleasant aroma arises from them as if somebody has perfumed them... sweet music can be heard in the background... just the music you like...

You know that your task is to assemble the big puzzle... though you feel you do not know where to begin... what to do and how?... there are so many pieces and how are you going to connect them?... you feel that your life is like this at the moment... lots of things are happening all the time... lots of emotions come up... your head is full of thoughts and you still do not know how everything links up... how to gather the pieces and build one picture from them... the picture of your life...

Perhaps you think you will not be able to assemble the puzzle... that it is too difficult and complicated... though something entices you to take one piece and start trying... to play with them... to examine what matches what and how... and you start playing with the pieces of the puzzle and you find a place for one piece and then another... and the feeling is good... very slowly you start to feel you are capable of doing it... that you can... that things are beginning to come together slowly and gradually... it makes you want to continue... you look at the pieces and think that if you knew in advance what the complete picture of the puzzle looked like, it would certainly be much easier to assemble it... at that moment you realize it is a magical puzzle, unique, for which you create the picture... you create the picture of your life as you want it to look... today, in the this magical house, you are given the opportunity to assemble it as you have dreamed of doing...

You can use the colors you want... you can add pieces as you like... perhaps you will see yourself in the picture... maybe other people... perhaps things that represent what you would like to see in your life... a feeling of excitement fills you when you think about what you would like in the picture of your life...

I will be quiet for about two minutes in order to allow you to assemble the picture you want of your life... you will hear my voice again in about two minutes...

You finish putting together the last pieces of your puzzle and can look at the picture that was produced... maybe you want to take out pieces that do not suit you... and perhaps you want to add a few other pieces... everything is possible in this picture... anything you want can go into it and there are no limitations... you can continue to decorate it in any way you want... in any manner that suits you, your life, and that makes you happy... all the pieces of the puzzle that you need are at your disposal...

And knowing this, you are invited to slowly return, to here, to this room, to your body, to this special day... you can lock the puzzle picture you created in your heart, and you can return to it and add more pieces at any time... and now you can begin to return... to move your hands and feet a little... and at your own pace... gently... slowly open your eyes... and return to here and now.

23. The Puzzle of My Life

24. New Growth

Category:
Finding direction

Who can benefit from this meditation?
People who have blossomed in a particular area and are beginning a new journey of learning.

Turning point

*After a difficult period,
When you felt nothing
is progressing,
Something in your life
changes now.
Something ends
and something new begins.
This is the time to adapt
to the cyclicality of life,
In which things come and go,
And to develop deep
insights into yourself.*

Allow yourself to find a comfortable position... feel the contact of your body on the mattress or on the chair... close your eyes... pay attention to the sounds outside and those you can hear inside the room... allow the noises to focus you on my voice... today you are going on a journey of growth and learning... and perhaps you are excited ahead of the journey... your subconscious is very wise and takes care of you, so you can loosen up knowing that it is doing its job in the best possible way... allow yourself to slowly and gradually get into a state of relaxation and calmness... to rest a little from everyday thoughts and activity and simply breathe deep... and listen...

Imagine yourself as a flower at the height of its flowering... this flower has got something that it does well, it has an ability that it brought to fruition... maybe in the professional domain... or in the realm of family... perhaps in a creative field that it has been involved in for a long time... perhaps in the field of sport... and perhaps in cooking... and perhaps in a completely different area... an area that only you know about...

Like the flower at the height of its flowering, you also feel certain and secure... you feel you have been in a learning process in one of your strong fields... perhaps deep down you feel you have got more to learn... though you know for certain that you have come a long way and that many people could benefit from the knowledge you have acquired...

This is a beautiful flower... it has magnificent petals... it has a strong, green stem... it has leaves to stabilize it... and you can see its unique color... and smell its pleasant fragrance... spring is evident around the flower, in the scenery... the sun gently warms the flower and a light breeze blows among its leaves...

At the same time, you feel a certain tiredness... the feeling that you have been flowering for some time and you are a little tired... you now are less excited by what you do... and other people are also less excited and perhaps got used to you...

You feel that there is another field you would like to try... another field that you are not yet familiar with and you would like to begin studying it... at the same time, you have doubts... you are not sure you have the strength to develop in a new field... yet when you think about it, something in you wants to try a new way nevertheless... to dare to develop in another direction... to flower once again... and again, the desire to renew is accompanied by hesitation, by doubt... and you are not certain you can make the whole journey again from the beginning... the sowing... the sprouting... and the renewed flowering...

And then, from within the doubt, you discover a voice that will not give up... and you follow it, you sow the little seed of a new beginning that comes out of your flower... you are not at all certain that this seed will survive... that it will take root... that it will dare... though by virtue of the bit in you that yearns and wants, you nevertheless sow another little seed... an attempt to do something in a new direction... maybe you read a bit about the field... maybe consult with somebody... perhaps you express you desire aloud for the first time...

And even if you are still doubtful, you notice that you have begun a new activity... perhaps only in the meanwhile... you have, however, started... and your heart is full of happiness at the thought that maybe you can really sprout the little seed and perhaps you can achieve renewed growth...

In your imagination, you fashion a new dream... and you can already see how the end of the process will look... and it gives you strength... perhaps reminding you of the past... some beginning of a dream you dreamed a long time ago... you have a certain inner belief that you are capable of it... and you are also reminded of an ancient saying: "Those who sow with tears, harvest with joy."

Good rains fall one day and irrigate your seeds... and you add special fertilizer... and the sun warms your seeds... and after a short while you notice a shoot has appeared and another one – the seeds you dispersed have suddenly turned into shoots... you feel great happiness when you see that your efforts and your persistence are starting to bear fruit... suddenly you are aware of something new... you begin to understand better...

You continue to grow and a small shoot turns into a stalk... that grows leaves... and a bud... and slowly and gradually it again turns into a beautiful flower... a flower that has undergone new growth... different growth... with a different color and different smell... and you are reminded of your previous flowering and you realize you have progressed and reached another circle of learning and creativity... an additional process of flowering-wilting-sowing-sprouting... a process that contains the cyclicality in nature... behold, you are flowering, this time in a different place... you know that in your new place you will be able to use all the previous knowledge you acquired as well as the new knowledge... and you know that you can always go on another new round of learning...

Knowing this fills you with joy and happiness like you experienced now... and with this feeling you begin to return to here, to this room... move your hands and feet a little... move your body gently... move your head comfortably from side to side... take a deep breath... and another breath... slowly open your eyes... and return at your own pace to normal wakefulness and full awareness... to here and now.

24. New Growth

25. The Spring of Calmness

Category:
Solving Problems

Who can benefit from this meditation?
People who are interested in loosening control and allowing themselves to be in the here and now.

Innocence

*Allow yourself to act innocently
and spontaneously now –
Without any intentions
or planning.
Let new things happen to you.
In this way unexpected things
with surprise you
as you make your way,
And the creativity
in you will awaken.*

Allow yourself to find a comfortable position... you will feel your body on the chair or on the mattress... relax your muscles a little... and slowly start feeling a sense of comfort... it is a time of rest for you... for the body... time that allows the head to free itself a little of thoughts and to loosen up... let your thoughts dissolve like light clouds moving in the sky with the wind, fading and disappearing... you can hear noises from outside and the music playing here in the room... allow yourself to focus on my voice... and feel how you get more and more comfortable from moment to moment...

You are in a beauty spot in nature, next to a spring... it is a beautiful spring, hidden in the undergrowth... you are alone next to the spring... at the same time you feel relaxed and calm... today you will be able to bathe in the spring... the spring of innocence...

It is a magical spring... when you get into it, you are only in the here and now... in this spring you can only be in the moment... the past and the future remain outside...

This spring reminds you how good it is to live in the moment... much of the time we are so busy planning the future or worrying about it... or lamenting the past, or perhaps yearning for it... that we forget how good it is to enjoy the moment... as it is... you know that soon you will be able to wrap yourself in the spring's pure water... you simply allow yourself to relax...

You prepare yourself for entering the water... slowly and gradually, you get into the spring... you feel the cool, pleasant water covering your body... you hear the relaxing sounds of the water... you can feel the tiny pebbles under your feet... how pleasant it is to swim in this spring... the water relaxes you... you are filled with growing calmness... the more time you are in the spring, so you are more relaxed... you feel how the thoughts remained outside... and here you can simply enjoy... simply relax... being in the "here and now" is very pleasant for you... the water washes you and gently cleans you...

You can pay attention to what you feel at the moment. What arises in you?... what flows from your spring?... what feeling occurs to you significantly?... let the feeling be, as it is... perhaps other feelings will arise... let them also be... you remain in the quiet spring, and the water continues to cover you more and more...

While you are relaxed and in this quiet, lots of ideas can appear... perhaps new insights will arise regarding this moment and its significance for you, solutions to questions and uncertainties can arise...

I will now be quiet for about two minutes and I will allow you to enjoy the calmness of the water... and the insights it brings... you will hear my voice again in about two minutes...

Now the time has come to leave the spring... you get out of the water... a large towel awaits you... you dry yourself and the pleasant rays of the sun warm your body... the innocence of the spring continues to accompany you... it enables you to be open to new good things that you are due to meet as you go on your way... perhaps meeting new people... perhaps new learning... perhaps some new creative activity, derived from a belief in your ability... you do not have to plan each step in your life... you can simply let the right things happen to you... and be open to new things... to things that come from the heart... to things that are good for you...

And with this good feeling, you begin to return to normal awareness here, to this room... you can move your hands and feet a little... move your body gently... move your head comfortably from side to side... take a deep breath... and another breath... slowly open your eyes... and return at your own pace to normal wakefulness and full awareness... to here and now.

25. The Spring of Calmness

26. Energy

Category:
Strengthening Resources

Who can benefit from this meditation?
People who feel the need to be charged with new energy.

Potential energy

*Take as a gift this stock of energy,
With which you can do anything and succeed.
Things become clear and new insights are gained.
All these enable you to reach peaks in your process of development.*

Allow yourself to find a comfortable position... you will feel your body on the chair or on the mattress... relax your muscles a little... and slowly start feeling a sense of comfort... it is a time of rest for you... for the body... time that allows the head to free itself a little of thoughts and to loosen up... you can hear noises from outside... allow yourself to focus on my voice... and feel how you get more and more comfortable from moment to moment...

Imagine yourself lying on a large couch... you are resting... the couch is in a spacious room... its walls are painted in colors you like and a large window lets in sunlight... a soft carpet is spread out on the floor... you let your body rest... to enjoy the softness of the large couch... the pleasant sound of music is playing... and you feel that you are relaxed and filled with calmness...

It is likely that of late you have felt emptied, tired, feeble... you feel there are lots of things you want to do... at the same time you lack energy... you lack the strength to execute things... to be able to change and advance things in your life... and you find this feeling difficult...

You discover a box on the table next to you... there are two sparkling stones in the box... and next to them a note on which is written: "these are your energy batteries... hold them and you will be filled with new energy... energy that will help you to do what you want and to succeed"...

You pick up the stones and feel them... their touch is cool and pleasant... you hold one stone in each hand and begin to feel how a wave of energy starts filling your body... first your hands... and then your arms... the energy rises and fills your chest... your stomach and back... and then it splits, one way to the legs and the other to your head... a pleasant warmth spreads slowly over your whole body... this is new energy filling all your organs... revitalizing energy...

You now feel you have strength to make changes... to advance plans... you get up from the comfortable couch and begin to do everything you have wanted to do for a long time and could not...

I will now be quiet for about two minutes and this will allow you to do everything you want and to progress... you will hear my voice in about two minutes...

You feel good and begin to do things... it fills you with a feel of renewal... satisfaction... the stones are full of energy and you can get more and more from them... as much as you want and need... you know you can also rest on the couch now and again and store new strength... and you discover that when you do things that are important to you something inside you opens up... you move forward... perhaps it takes time to get accustomed to this... but you know that you will always be able to be charged with energy and continue...

You notice that the stones have changed color... they are now blue... the color of healing... you sit down on the couch and hold one in each hand... and the healing energy goes through your body exactly as the previous energy did... something gets re-balanced... something in you is healed... you discover that the stones have immediate healing powers – every ache or problem is charged with blue light, healing light, and it vanishes... you feel that from moment to moment, from day to day you will be able to feel better and better...

The stones stay with you... and they have the ability to change color according to your needs... and to be filled with different types of energy... you know you can be helped by them whenever you need them... they are here for you, with their blessed energy.

And with this good feeling you begin to return to normal awareness here, to this room... you can move your hands and feet a little... move your body gently... move your head comfortably from side to side... take a deep breath... and another breath... slowly open your eyes... and return at your own pace to normal wakefulness and full awareness... to here and now.

26. Energy

27. The Kingdom of Good Nutrition

Category:
Strengthening Resources

Who can benefit from this meditation?
People who are interested in eating while paying attention to their body.

Nutrition

*This is the time to examine how you
operate in your environment:
Who feeds you
and with what?
Did you get the things
you need?
Who do you feed?
Are they worthy of your feeding?
Your good feeding of yourself
and the environment,
Will permit good fortune
and growth.*

Allow yourself to find a comfortable position... you will feel your body on the chair or on the mattress... relax your muscles a little... and slowly start feeling a sense of comfort... it is a time of rest for you... for the body... time that allows the head to free itself a little of thoughts and to loosen up... let your thoughts dissipate like light clouds in the sky that move with the wind, dissolve and disappear... you can hear noises from outside... allow yourself to focus on my voice... and feel how you get more and more comfortable from moment to moment...

Imagine yourself to be a king or queen sitting on the throne in your palace... the palace is beautiful... it is designed exactly according to your taste... pleasant music is heard in it... there is something very relaxed and calm about your palace... something that arouses respect...

You can feel your beautiful, royal clothes... they are made of shiny silk cloth... you are sitting on the throne at a time when you are just the weight you want to be at, with the look you want... wearing clothes of the exact size you want to wear... opposite you there is a large mirror you stand in front of and look... perhaps it is hard for you to believe, though you are exactly the weight you have dreamed of... and you look fabulous... radiant... your hair is beautifully styled... you look just wonderful...

There is an abundance of food in your kingdom... nutritious food... fattening food... food that you like... food that you like less... every morning you are grateful for the abundance of food bestowed on you... and you are happy to be in a kingdom that has such great abundance...

At the same time, you, and only you, decide what food enters your palace... each morning you carry out a thorough examination of each and every bit of food... and only food that suits you passes the test and enters the palace... you examine its nutrient value... the amount of calories... how essential it is... perhaps it is food you love and its nutrient value is low, then it visits your kingdom less frequently... or each time a little...

Three things help your royal sorting job... these are your secret resources... you consult them when you are deciding what food to permit into your palace... these resources are sewn onto your royal clothing... they are three shiny buttons... you feel them each time you deliberate...

The first button is sewn on close to your heart... this is the button of self-love... it reminds you that you love yourself and your body... and that you know to fill your body only with good things...

Every time you press this button, your heart fills with love for yourself... you forgive yourself for certain deeds... and you remember the good deeds you have done... all the good things in you... you now fill your heart only with your good things... and you can really feel in your body your love for yourself...

The second button is in the stomach region... it is the button of self-feeding... it allows you to feel your ability to feed yourself in the right, good way... so that you feel good with yourself... so that you receive exactly what you need from yourself and from others... you will be able to feed others well... being attentive to their needs... and now, being attentive to your needs... you fill yourself with the ability to feed yourself well...

The third button is close to your neck... it is the button of your self-expression and creativity... by touching this button you can arouse your ability to express your needs... to be filled with the ability to create the reality of your life in the way you would like it to be... the ability to raise ideas... thoughts in your creative way... and put them into practice... you fill yourself with the ability to create and express your will...

When you are deciding which foods come into your palace and which don't, you press on the different buttons and they help you to love yourself... to feed yourself well... to express yourself and to create the reality of your life in the best possible way for you...

From day to day you are better able to feel your ability to choose what is good for you... what is right for you... how to feed yourself... you feel you will be able to look just like the king or queen you are... to feel like them... you will be able to choose which foods enter your palace and which ones remain outside... you have plenty of resources to do this...

And with this clear understanding, you can begin to return to here, to this room... you can move your hands and feet a little... move your body gently... move your head comfortably from side to side... take a deep breath... and another breath... slowly open your eyes... and return at your own pace to normal wakefulness and full awareness... to here and now.

27. The Kingdom of Good Nutrition

28. The Chore Sack

Category:
Solving Problems

Who can benefit from this meditation?
People who are very busy and bothered and are looking for a bit of quiet and tranquility.

Too much

*Many events in your life are reaching their peak.
Too many things are happening at once,
And they demand a lot of your strength.
Evaluate the situation.
Set an order of priorities,
And find in yourself the strength,
That will allow you to get through this period successfully.*

Allow yourself to find a comfortable position and take a deep breath... and another breath... pay attention to your breath... is it fast or slow?... does it move easily or does it encounter a difficulty in a particular place in the body?... pay attention to the flow of air from outside to your body and from your body back outside... and notice how focusing on your breathing allows you to relax slowly...

With the fast pace of everyday life, sometimes we forget to breathe... for you this is an opportunity to breathe deeper, to breathe comfortably and let yourself rest... to loosen up... let your breathing take you deep inside yourself... to experience the most basic existence... to breathing... to the body's wonderful ability to feed itself with oxygen all the time... and you take a breath and another breath... and permit yourself more and more calmness...

Imagine yourself standing on the sidewalk of a wide street... you are tired and you lean against the wall of a building... you watch the people passing by and see them behaving like you behave every day... they are busy, running from place to place, and you look at them and realize that you also run around like them... you also have lots of places to get to... like them you want to accomplish more and more, you want to run quickly... though something is stopping you now...

There is a large, heavy sack placed on your back... it makes it difficult for you to move... makes it difficult for you to walk... it contains everything you have to accomplish and do... you are carrying all your assignments on your back... they make it difficult for you to advance... make it difficult for you to run as you would like, if only you could...

You can feel the great burden resting on your shoulders... a very significant burden... you decide, regardless of the time pressure and everything you have to do, to stop for a moment... to cross over to the park on the other side of the street... to put the sack down beside you... and sit down on a bench... to let yourself rest... it is not easy for you to relax and feel calm, because you know it will be difficult for you to manage everything... though you simply have to stop... to rest a little...

You open the sack and look at what you have to do... perhaps some of the things are connected to work... some to home... some to family... there are so many things that you struggle to count them... the sack is full of chores... you begin to arrange the chores next to you... you check what is more important and what less important... what you can delay a little... and leave in the park for the moment... so that you will find it easier to carry the sack...

I will now be quiet for the next two minutes and allow you to sort out the chores very well... you will hear my voice again in two minutes...

You leave some things in the park... relinquish them, and some chores you put in a box at the side... some of the things will wait here for you at a later date... and you can give some of the chores to somebody else to do... you write down the person's name... you take away with you only those things that you have to take now... and go on your way... it is much easier for you carrying fewer things... it is much more comfortable... and simple...

You feel you can learn to let go of some of the things... to relinquish... to examine what is really important to you and that you have to do, and what somebody else can do for you... you feel how you are starting to feel calm... relaxed... the thoughts are managing to rest a little and are becoming clearer... you can begin to relax... and when you walk along the path in the park you are suddenly freed to look around you... there are beautiful flowers beside the path... you can smell their aroma in the air... butterflies pass by and you hear the chirping of birds around... when you are running you do not notice the beautiful sights along the path... and now, you are walking with a lighter sack, you can enjoy the calm and the quiet...

You understand how you can be freer as the days pass... you can reduce your chores and enjoy everyday things more and more... and from your free time... slowly you will get used to resting a little and relaxing... it is a pleasant feeling when you can permit yourself to relax... to walk instead of running... this feeling fills your whole body... and it will soon be time to return... allow yourself to retain the feeling of lightness on the way back, too...

And with this feeling, you can begin to return to here, to this room... you can move your hands and feet a little... move your body gently... move your head comfortably from side to side... take a deep breath... and another breath... slowly open your eyes... and return at your own pace to normal wakefulness and full awareness... to here and now.

28. The Chore Sack

29. Diving Deep

Category:
Strengthening Resources

Who can benefit from this meditation?
People who are interested to delve into the depths of their soul.

Danger

*When water flows in a torrent,
You are in danger of being
carried towards an abyss.
You will need
all your strength,
To protect yourself.
The danger allows you to find
inner strength,
That you did not know existed.
Use this time for growth and
toughening.*

Allow yourself to find a comfortable position... you will feel your body on the chair or on the mattress... relax your muscles a little... and slowly start feeling a sense of comfort... it is a time of rest for you... for the body... time that allows the head to free itself a little of thoughts and to loosen up... let your thoughts dissipate like light clouds in the sky that move with the wind, dissolve and disappear... you can hear noises from outside... and the music playing here in the room... allow yourself to focus on my voice... and feel how you get more and more comfortable from moment to moment...

You have reached a special beach, and you can see the sea as far as the horizon... it is an exceptionally pleasant day... with your feet you can feel the bright sand on the beach... you can see the palm trees growing all around... you can hear the swish of the waves and the sound of the seagulls... you are a little excited... because you know that today you are going to dive into the depths... and you have already put on your diving suit...

Behold, your instructor, who will accompany you on your dive, is approaching... he reaches you and you can see that he is a person in whose company you feel safe and can rely on... he is wearing a diving suit and has brought along very special oxygen cylinders: the oxygen cylinders contain curiosity, courage and daring... and they will help you to dive and to explore the depths...

Exploring the depths of the sea is like exploring the depths of the soul... perhaps danger lurks in diving to the depths of the soul... maybe you will find things that have been repressed and it is difficult to cope with them... troubling emotions... painful memories... at the same time, sometimes you can find real treasures there... important insights... happy memories... times of overcoming difficulties... deep inside yourself you can find the strength to assist you on your way...

The diving instructor invites you to begin your journey... and you notice a boat waiting for you near the beach... you climb onto the boat and see that its bottom is made of glass... this boat lets you see the depths of the sea... you sit down in the boat and look... the water is clear... schools of small and big fish swim back and forth under the boat... you can hear the sound of the waves... and feel the wind blowing... and you feel you want to dive into the water... to actually feel it, yourself... and not just through the glass screen...

The instructor gets into the boat and begins to row it... you sit comfortably and get addicted to the waves moving it... the rolling of the water relaxes you more and more... you move further from the coast, and the instructor invites you to jump into the water with him... you are a little worried about doing so, though anyway, you adjust the oxygen cylinders and jump in after him... the water is cool and pleasant... you pluck up courage and dive deeper and deeper... going down into the sea... and the deeper you go in the depths of the sea, the more calm and relaxed you feel... a feeling of comfort spreads around your body...

In the ocean depths you discover new, amazing things... you gain insights that can only be gained by diving deep inside... diving into the depths of the soul... right inside you... maybe insights into your past... maybe insights regarding your future... maybe about your present situation... diving deep allows you to relax and to observe the depths of your soul... inside yourself... you find special powers inside yourself, powers whose existence you may have forgotten about...

I will now be quiet for about three minutes and will allow you to gain the insights... you will hear my voice again in about three minutes...

And with the insights that arose in you, you observe the fish... the seaweed... the coral... the instructor invites you to start moving up... slowly, slowly... on every dive you need to go back up at a very slow pace... you go higher and higher until you reach the surface of the water... once on the surface you notice you have moved away from the boat... it frightens you a little, though you trust yourself and the instructor to be able to swim to it... you begin to swim back... you find it hard to advance because the waves are washing you back, and the fear arises again, and then you remember that you have oxygen cylinders that contain courage and daring... you use all your strength and advance towards the boat... you reach it... the instructor offers you a hand and helps you to climb aboard...

On the way back to the beach you notice that the water is calm and pleasant, the murmur of the waves is light and quiet... you feel you have the ability to cope and to dive down deep... to examine yourself and others... to gain insight... and even if the water carries you away sometimes, you have at your disposal all the power to contend with the obstacles... as time passes you will be able to overcome the difficulties and find your way to surmount them...

You slowly begin to return to here, to this room... to your beach, to this special day... the day on which you dived into the depths of your soul and found strength and insights there... lock the new pictures as well as your insights of the dive into your heart and let them lead you forwards...

And with this knowledge and these insights, you can move your hands and feet a little... move your body gently... move your head comfortably from side to side... take a deep breath... and another breath... slowly open your eyes... and return at your own pace to normal wakefulness and full awareness... to here and now.

29. Diving Deep

30. Shared Fire

Category:
Strengthening Resources

Who can benefit from this meditation?
People who are interested
in initiating collaborations.

Synergy

*Collaboration will produce
better results,
Than anything you do
on your own,
Collaborate with yourself
and with others.
Listen to the sounds
of the universe,
In order to collaborate
with them, too.*

Allow yourself to find a comfortable position... feel your body touching the mattress or the chair... close your eyes... pay attention to the noises from outside and those that can be heard in the room... let the noises allow you to focus on my voice... today you are going on a journey of growth and learning... perhaps you are excited ahead of it... your subconscious is very wise and takes care of you, and you can relax knowing that it is doing the job in the best way possible... allow yourself slowly, slowly and gradually to enter into relaxation and calmness... rest a little from the thoughts and from the whole day's activity and breathe deeply... and listen...

You are standing in the heart of a forest... in a clearing in the forest... in a place where the trees give way to fresh grass... it is the end of a pleasant summer day and the sun is slowly setting through the trees... the sun's setting instill calmness in you... it is getting dark, although you feel protected and secure... you feel that as the suns sets you become more relaxed...

And you want to light a campfire... to introduce fresh fire into your life and light up the darkness that is about to descend on the forest... you search for a place where you can safely light the fire... a special place where the fire can burn... it is a place where it will be pleasant for you to sit near the fire and enjoy its warmth and light... you clear a space... the pleasant smell of the soil rises into your nose... and you can hear the twittering of birds preparing for the night's sleep...

You gather twigs and branches for the fire... the last rays of the sun light your way and direct you to places where you can find wood for the fire... you can hear the rustle of leaves under your feet... and can feel the pleasant breeze blowing at this time of the evening...

After you have gathered all the wood and twigs and placed them in the fire's special place, you arrange them to make them easy to light... you find a box of matches and begin to light the fire... perhaps you need a few attempts till the fire catches alight and maybe you manage to light it first time... fine smoke arises from the little fire... you can smell it... you see the burning flames... and you hear the sounds of the fire...

Making the fire makes you very happy... you get excited... something new has been lit in your life... you want this fire to continue to burn for a long time... the fire of your ideas... your learning... fire that you create and it is unique to you... its colors are extraordinary... yellow... orange... blue and purple...

You add wood to the fire... and collect more wood... the fire burns and lights up your surroundings and your way... it warms you... at the same time, you feel it would be good if you had people with whom to share the fire... who would help you guard the blaze... more people who could sit with you around the fire... get warm together from the heat of the fire...

I will now be quiet for about two minutes, during which you can decide which people you would invite to join you at your campfire... at your fire... and how they could help you preserve the light... the fire... they could either be people you know or people you want to get to know... perhaps spiritual guides you have... invite them to join you... imagine them joining you... you will hear my voice again in about two minutes...

And now that you have found suitable people to help guard the fire... you sit together and get warm... perhaps you chat among yourselves or maybe sing... perhaps you create a division of roles to guard the fire and see that it is just the right size for you... too big a fire can be dangerous... as too small a fire can go out... allow yourselves to find ways to keep the fire the size you want...

And from sitting like this around the fire with your partners, you feel how, as time passes, the collaboration between you produces wonderful results... exactly as you saw in your dreams... the shared fire shines for everybody and creates combined strength... shared energy... and common abilities that are greater than the personal ability of each, individual person... and with this magical blaze, you notice that the dawn is breaking through the trees of the forest... the morning is different from yesterday's... it is a morning that harbors new beginnings... new collaborations...

And as the sun's first rays reach the clearing in the forest... and with the arrival of the forest ranger at you campfire, you leave the fire in his hands and slowly begin to return to your body and to this room... you can move your hands and feet a little... move your body gently... move your head comfortably from side to side... take a deep breath... and another breath... slowly open your eyes... and return at your own pace to normal wakefulness and full awareness... to here and now.

30. Shared Fire

31. The Magnet

Category:
Strengthening Resources

Who can benefit from this meditation?
People who are interested in attracting into their lives the things they want most, and are most appropriate.

Attraction

You are strongly attracted to the matter,
You are busy with at the moment,
And it is attracted to you.
Let the attraction occur and influence you,
And that way you will be able to tell if it is good for you.
It is an opportunity to examine what things you attract to your life,
And how they can affect you later.

Allow yourself to find a comfortable position... feel your body touching the mattress or the chair... this is a time of rest for you... for your body... a time to let your head rest from thoughts and relax... slowly and gradually your thoughts dissolve like light clouds scattering in the wind on a summer day... you will be able to hear noises from outside... allow yourself to focus on my voice... and feel how you feel more and more relaxed and calm as time passes...

And now imagine yourself in a beautiful house, designed exactly according to your taste... you are sitting in the lounge on a soft couch... looking with satisfaction at the pleasant house... a pleasant tune is playing in the background... the sounds relax you and create calmness in you... there is a small table next to you, on which is placed a wrapped present...

And you know this present is for you... you hold it and feel the shiny paper... you wonder what it can be and from whom it comes... and you begin to open it... first the ribbon... afterwards the paper... and inside you discover a little box...

You open the box, inside which is a magnet... a simple, square magnet... however, you realize that it is not so simple, it is a special magnet... it is a magnet that enables you to attract to your life only things you are interested in... only things you want... you hold the magnet in your hands, excited by this magic... and start to ponder about things you would like to attract into your life... (wait a moment)

It's certain there are people you would like to get to know... perhaps you want to attract positive thoughts... happy emotions... magic moments... and perhaps experiences and adventures, like travelling round the world... perhaps learning new fields... or perhaps simply to attract moments of rest in which you can let go a bit and rest... read a good book... or anything else...

I will now be quiet for about two minutes and will allow you to imagine, to discover and find what things you would like to attract into your life... you will hear my voice again in about two minutes...

You are still holding the magnets, and you can attract into your life the things you want... you can think about them and feel how the magnet helps you to pull them to you... more and more... anything you want you can attract to you... you have the ability to bring into your life lots of good things... things and people who will be good for you, who will enrich your personality and your life... who will bring you happiness and love... you have the ability at any time to choose what you attract to yourself and what not...

You are happy with the present you received and you would like to keep the magnet close to your heart... you slowly shrink it until it reaches the size to fit your heart... and then you simply put it in your heart... the magnet merges with the heart... now you can continue attracting, any day, by means of your heart, the things you want to attract... allow yourself to check what and who you attract and why... behind the people and the situations we attract into our lives there are often stunning lessons hidden... check what you can learn from each situation... and allow yourself to go forward...

The magnet is in your heart... and your magnetic ability is growing from day to day... perhaps at the moment you feel your ability to attract good things to your life is minimal... at the same time, it will increase as time passes... you will be able to attract whatever you want... the magnet will serve you in all situations... feel the attraction occurring in your heart... let it gain strength slowly and gradually... from today you will be able to touch your heart whenever you want to recall your ability to attract...

And with this ability to attract, you are invited to return to here, to this room... you can move your hands and feet a little... move your body gently... move your head comfortably from side to side... take a deep breath... and another breath... slowly open your eyes... and return at your own pace to normal wakefulness and full awareness... to here and now.

31. The Magnet

32. A Letter from the Inner Child

Category:
Past

Who can benefit from this meditation?
People who are interested in recalling pleasant, affirming memories from their childhood, and to gain strength from them.

Continuity

*At this time you can recover all
the good things,
You collected from your
childhood:
The good qualities, the
amazing abilities,
The values and everything you
have had for a long time.
All these will help you bring
new things into your life.*

Allow yourself to find a comfortable position... feel the touch of your body on the mattress or on the chair... relax your muscles slightly... slowly begin to feel comfortable... this is a time of rest for you... for your body... a time to let your head rest from thoughts and relax... let your thoughts dissolve like light clouds moving in the wind on a summer day, dissolving and disappearing... you will be able to hear noises from outside and the music playing here in the room... allow yourself to focus on my voice... and feel how you feel more and more relaxed as time passes...

Imagine yourself standing on a hill overlooking a lovely valley... it is a clear day, a spring sun is shining... the sky is light blue... you stand and observe the valley and it has something that attracts you... you can hear the wind blowing and can feel its caressing touch on your face and hair... and with this pleasant feeling you allow yourself to relax more and more...

You begin to go down into the valley... the walk is pleasant and easy, and as you go down you feel the calmness spread in your body... you continue to advance and to observe the valley, and suddenly you realize that there is something familiar about this valley from your childhood... you descend lower and lower, and now you are in the valley proper... you look around and enjoy its magical view...

A few yards away you notice a mail box that arouses your curiosity... you approach it and hesitate about whether to open it or not... because you do not know to whom it belongs... to your surprise you discover that your name is written on it in big letters...

You are surprised to see that the envelope looks familiar to you... its smell is also familiar and you do not know where from... your name is written on the letter in a child's handwriting... you look at the name and recognize your writing from the age of about eight, nine...

You open the envelope and look at the letter... you sit down on a comfortable stone under a tree and begin to read... you realize that the letter was written for you from the child you used to be, in grade three or four... you read the letter and become very emotional... the child you were has written to you about the things you liked doing... about his/her dreams... about his/her friends... about his/her happy times... perhaps he/she describes his/her daily routine...

I will now be quiet for about two minutes so that you can read the letter... and perhaps see the child's daily routine just like a movie... in about two minutes you will hear my voice...

You have finished reading and are flooded with lots of memories from your childhood... you are emotional... perhaps you have received a message or an insight from the child you were... something that can help you today... maybe the child is pointing you in a particular direction that will enable you to realize your dream...

A childlike ray of light comes out from the letter and enters your heart... a feeling of warmth fills you... it is a sign for you to remember the wishes and dreams of the child you were... to experience the child who is still in your heart... while you are absorbed in your memories and thoughts about the child in you... you fold the letter and put it in the envelope and keep it with you, in case you want to read it again...

Slowly, slowly... with very soft steps... you begin to return to the hill, knowing that in the future you can come back here... to the beautiful, familiar valley... and maybe you will receive more letters from the child you were... if you want, you can write letters to him/her, to the child, and tell him/her about your life... to tell him/her about what has happened since then and how you coped with various things... you get back to the top of the hill with a feeling of fullness and joy...

And with this very special feeling, you are invited to slowly and gradually return to here, to this room... you can move your hands and feet a little... take a deep breath... slowly open your eyes... and slowly, slowly return... at your own pace... to normal awareness... to here and now.

32. A Letter from the Inner Child

33. Time to Retreat

Category:
Solving Problems

Who can benefit from this meditation?
People who are following a certain path and realize they have to retreat and follow a different path – to make a change.

Retreat

*It is time to retreat –
from strength
and not from weakness,
Because battles
are useless now.
Retreat in order to examine your
thought patterns,
And investigate why things are
not working out as you want.
Retreat will bring success.*

A llow yourself to find a comfortable position... and give yourself the opportunity to rest... your body works hard, exerts itself the whole day and this is an opportunity to let it relax a little... when you are comfortable on the chair or mattress feel how all the places in your body where tension has built up loosen up and slowly relax... it is a pleasant feeling of release... allow yourself to take a deep breath and another breath and let the air flow through your body... the air flows through the open place and sometimes has difficulty flowing through the blocked places... bring awareness to these places and allow them to open up... take another breath... and another... feel how the air brings serenity and calmness into the body, to each and every corner... and you connect more and more to the quiet in you...

Now you are on a journey towards the peak of a mountain... it is a pleasant day and the sun warms you as you walk... you are climbing up the mountainside... climbing up... it is a steep incline and you are panting a bit... though you continue on... you think about going down and giving up... however, something tells you that if you have already started out on this road, it is worthwhile continuing on it... something in you wants to continue... and something wants to return...

And you keep going... up and up... on the most suitable way for you... no giving up... keep going... you have reached a high, wide cliff... there is a magnificent view from it... you look around you and see how beautiful it is below... you see the sea... the dunes around it and little houses... there is a strong wind blowing on your face...

And you want to continue climbing from the cliff to the mountain peak and try to find your way forward... you try one way and it is too steep... you try another way, and it is too full of undergrowth... and third way is littered with stones... all paths are blocked... the only possibility is to go back the way you came... in other words, to go down...

You are disappointed that you cannot continue... on the one hand, you very much wanted to reach the top, the peak... on the other hand, you are also happy... the constant climb tired you... and the descent seems easier... and yet, you are a little disappointed in yourself about not finding a way to continue... and now you have to return...

You check the possible paths again... try to find a possible way for you... finally you decide to go back... the descent is indeed easier... you can see the view that was behind you before... the pleasant breeze helps you on your way... blows with you... suddenly you notice a birds' nest with chicks... the chicks chirp happily when their mother brings them food... you have a feeling of warmth at the sight of the bird and her chicks...

You continue to descend and feel how the descent calms you... you begin to acknowledge the fact that the best way was to go back... to the place you set out from... you learn from this journey that sometimes we choose a particular path and it does not serve us... and it is okay to decide to go back and retreat... to go back to the starting point and rethink what the right path is for us...

You continue to descend... more relaxed and calm as time passes... you are full of perfection... the view accompanies you all along the way... and you discover a small cave on your way... it seems cool and pleasant... you go in to rest... sit down on a stone... and feel it is a unique cave... it is filled with a pale blue light... a healing, calming light... light that enables you to heal... and a feeling of perfection...

You remain in the cave and allow yourself to receive the pale blue healing light... still feeling at one with yourself... you feel how the pale blue light healed your whole body... allow yourself to be filled up with the pale blue light... feel how it fills your body... how pleasant it is to feel it... you take a deep breath, get up and leave... you return to the point where you started the journey... when you return to it you know you can think later about and understand what new path suits you best... the way you want to tramp... perhaps you already know what the right way is and perhaps you knew all along and now you allow yourself to go along the way that best suits you... as time passes you will be able to connect more and more to your heart, knowing which paths are good and suitable for you...

And with this understanding, you begin to return here... take a deep breath... you have embarked on a thought-provoking journey, and now the time has arrived to begin to return... it is a good feeling... special... and with this special feeling you are invited to begin to return slowly and gradually to here, to this room... move your hands and feet a little... take a deep breath, gently open your eyes... and slowly, slowly you return... at your own pace... to normal awareness... to here and now.

33. Time to Retreat

34. The Room of Strength

Category:
Past

Who can benefit from this meditation?
People who are interested in recalling their inner strengths and to be assisted by them on the way ahead.

Great strength

You possess great strength,
Strength that can help you
on your way.
Check if you are using your
strength in a smart way.
Use your strength to advance
a positive goal.
Helping others by using your
strength will benefit you.

Allow yourself to close your eyes... find a comfortable position for your body... you can listen to the voices from outside and the voices in the room... take pleasure in the music playing in the background... and focus on my voice... you are likely to be busy with thoughts... lots of things occupy you... allow yourself to loosen up a little from the thoughts, know that you can return to them afterwards... try to focus your pupils in the direction of your nose – it helps your thoughts to rest... relax slowly and go into the quiet inside yourself... deep inside... take a deep breath and another one and feel how the calmness seeps inside, further into your body...

You are in a multi-storied building... on the fifth floor... it is a large building in the city... you have got to the building today in order to investigate something important to you and to understand... what the secret of your strength is... you know you have the strength that can help you on your way... and perhaps you feel that you have not used it for a long time... you are feeling that you could have done a lot with your strength... at the same time, you have forgotten what its source is...

You decide to use the elevator and go down to the ground floor of the building... there you will be able to discover the secret of your strength... its source... you enter the elevator and press the button "Room of Strength"... the elevator begins to descend... it is lit by a pleasant light... calm music can be heard in it... elevator music... something about the descent of the elevator instills you with calmness and serenity... you feel very safe inside it... the elevator continues to descend, and as it descends you relax more and more... and you feel a pleasing excitement ahead of the visit to the room of strength...

The elevator stops and announces, "The strength corridor"... you exit the elevator and stride down the corridor... you see photographs hanging on the wall... photographs of your successes... photographs of you as a toddler managing to walk for the first time... photographs of you saying your first word... and in first grade succeeding to read and write... and photographs of good friends... photographs of you passing a test... photographs of you helping someone... and many other photographs of you succeeding during the course of your life... there are words written on the photographs that mention abilities and strengths that you know in your heart you have...

You continue along the strength corridor... it has a slight slope and it takes you down to the room of strength... the room is totally white... lots of candles are burning in it and light it up... you can smell the pleasant scent of the candles... it is a well-lit room... and the light in it relaxes you... instills comfort and calm in you... there is a round table covered with a white tablecloth standing in the middle of the room... there is a large crystal ball on the tablecloth...

You know you will find the secret of your strength in this crystal ball... the things that will help you to advance and realize your ambitions... soon you will discover what is hidden in you... perhaps it is a rare talent... perhaps a good quality... maybe an outstanding ability, like the ability to help... or another ability... every person has inner strength... and it is different for every person... even if it is difficult to see, it always exists... and today you will find your special, personal strength... your amazing powers...

Now you approach the table... you are about to look into the crystal ball and with its help discover what your unique strength is... you look into the crystal ball... I will be quiet for about two minutes and allow you to see what is reflected in the crystal ball... perhaps you will hear a voice telling you things... you will hear my voice again in about two minutes...

A white light emerges from the crystal ball and fills your body... the crystal ball charges your body with a lot of strength... strength you will be able to use to advance goals that are important to you... that will do you good... you feel how the white light gently enters your body and also enshrouds it like a white halo... allow yourself to feel the powers that fill you... breathe the white light into your body... more and more...

And the time has come to continue... you begin to leave the room of strength and return via the corridor of strength... you notice the change that has taken place in your photographs... more powerful events from your life appear in them, events in which you succeeded... you encouraged a friend... you were praised at work... and perhaps you can see yourself in the photograph in which you managed to create something, to bake or cook something tasty...

You go up in the illuminated elevator... and you discover that instead of stopping on the fifth floor, the elevator continues to take you up and up... to the tenth floor... you realize the crystal ball has filled you with great strength... that enables you to advance more and more... at the tenth floor you exit the elevator and find yourself on a large balcony... here, at a great height, you can connect to your great strength... one that can at any time continue to develop... take a breath and fill yourself with this feeling... a bridge leads from the balcony, by way of which you can go outside and make your way back...

And from this bridge... with you full of strength... when new powers and old-new abilities have arisen in you... you are invited to return... at a pace that suits you... to here, to this room... you slowly begin to return to normal awareness and normal wakefulness... to feel your body again... move your hands a little... and your feet... open your eyes and return, at your own pace... to here and now.

34. The Room of Strength

35. Inner Light

Category:
Strengthening Resources

Who can benefit from this meditation?
People who are interested in gaining strength from their inner light.

Progress

*Something inside you
is glowing,
And projecting light onto all
those around you.
You progress quickly and
advance many others.
You are also progressing in your
social standing.
In this way you approach
your destiny.*

Allow yourself to find a comfortable position... close your eyes... pay attention to the sounds from outside and those that can be heard in the room... allow the noises to focus your attention on my voice... today you are embarking on a journey of growth and learning... perhaps you are excited ahead of the journey... your subconscious is very smart and you can rely on it, loosen up and know that it will do the job in the best possible way... allow yourself to slowly, slowly and gradually enter into serenity, to calmness... rest a little from the thoughts and from activity and simply breathe deeply... and listen...

And now imagine yourself walking in a little alley in a town... the houses around you are built from stone that looks ancient and charming... pots of plants that are filled with flowers of a wide range of colors hang in the windows... this alleyway is pleasant... through the house windows you can hear conversations taking place and feel that there are people living in this town... you can hear the laughter of children... you can smell the aromas of home cooking... it is an ancient city, built long ago... and you are pleased to see that life goes on in it now...

The alleys are shaded and pleasant... and a light breeze musses your hair... and you continue to ramble at your leisure... you notice that there are galleries and stores in the alley... you stop and look at the art and craft work... and there is something relaxing about this window shopping... something that instills calmness and serenity in you... it is so pleasant to walk around this town now...

You go down the alley steps and continue looking at the stores... as you descend you relax more and more... you know that you will soon see something very interesting in one of the stores and you feel that one particular store at the bottom is really calling you and inviting you to come... you continue to descend until you reach the store... "The Light in You" is written on a small sign... carefully, you open a small door... and go down a few steps until you are in the store itself...

Surrounding you are candles, lamps, oil lamps and chandeliers, all radiating light... the store is full of light... and pleasant aromas rise in your nose... the scent of the candles... the atmosphere of the store is very pleasant... an elderly saleslady with a soft smile comes up to you and begins to explain to you about the many lighting options there are in the store... she tells you that these are internal lighting units and you may choose from among them the light with which to shine light...

You choose a small lamp whose light gets stronger all the time... slowly, slowly and gradually... you feel this is the pace that suits you... which is also the way you want to shine light... where the light grows continuously... you know that the light that comes out of you can also light the way for other people... it is very significant light...

The saleslady takes the little lamp that you have chosen from the shelf... and you notice that instead of wrapping it for you she takes the light from the lamp and slowly transfers it to your body... from the top of your head... via your face... neck... you feel how the light in you moves towards your chest... the stomach... pelvis and down your legs to your feet...

Your whole body sends out light... radiates good light around... light that is now inside you... part of you... it increases together with your development process... it is pleasant to have the light residing inside your body... it relaxes you...

And with the light filling you, you get ready to leave the store... you happily bid the saleslady farewell... she invites you to visit the store anytime... if you need another light... she teaches you how you can increase the inner light you now have... inside you... by means of a feeling of self-love... each time you feel the need to charge the light inside you, you can do it by loving yourself... be forgiving, learn to accept yourself... in this way you will refill with stronger and stronger light... the saleslady asks you to remember that self-love is essential for your development and progress...

You thank the saleslady and return to the alley... you feel uniquely happy... go up the steps, and continue to walk along the way you came... and soon you will begin to return from the ancient town to here... with the new light inside, you slowly begin to return to here, to this room... to normal awareness... to normal wakefulness... you still feel the light inside you, casting light from inside you outwards... you begin to move your feet a little... and your hands... open your eyes at your own pace and return to here and now.

35. Inner Light

36. *Growing Towards the Light*

Category:
Solving Problems

Who can benefit from this meditation?
People contending with criticism.

Criticism

*At this time you are exposed
to criticism,
And you will find it difficult
to progress in any direction.
Pretend to accept things as they
are, and do not confront.
At the same time, be faithful
to the things,
You believe in
wholeheartedly.*

Allow yourself to close your eyes and find a comfortable position... feel the contact of your body with the chair or the mattress... and the temperature of the room... perhaps you can hear voices from outside and the voices and the sounds here in the room... allow yourself to focus on my voice and slowly connect to a quiet place inside you... to the quiet in you... take a deep breath... and another one... feel how the air enters the body and brings quiet and calmness... and the air that leaves the body enables you to release everything that you no longer need...

Imagine yourself to be a young sapling planted in the heart of a large forest... not long ago you came out of the ground... and you joined the trees of the forest... you can imagine which tree you are a sapling of... and which other trees grow in the forest with you...

There are many trees in the forest... most of them emerged from the bowels of the earth a long time ago and grew a large, wide trunk... lots of dense branches... lovely green leaves... you look at the big trees... you can hear the rustle of the leaves in the wind... the leaves are so dense that they block the sunlight from you... their bulk makes it dark for you... and you struggle to see the sky through their tops...

You feel afraid and worried: will you succeed in getting as big as the other trees?... will you manage to reach the sky with your head?... do you have the courage to grow to such heights?... to raise yourself like them?... perhaps the trees around you sometimes give you the feeling that you cannot get big like them... that you are still missing something in order to be able to develop so well...

Allow yourself, pretty little sapling, to grow at your own pace... in your own way... in directions that are right for you... in time it is likely you will hear criticism of the way you are growing... sometimes criticism can be a gift for you... listening to constructive criticism can assist your growth process... you can always detect criticism that boosts you... at the same time, allow yourself to be connected to your ability to grow as you are... in your way... even if other people think there are only certain ways that make it possible to succeed... you know inside yourself and are sure you can operate in your own way... allow yourself to feel this feeling... feel in your heart your ability to succeed in your own way... let this feeling fill your heart... feel it spreading in your hair, slowly and gradually... take a deep breath and let it seep in... more and more...

When you are connected to your ability to succeed in your own way you notice that something has changed... your young sapling grew and sprouted beautiful branches... exceptional branches... the trunk grew and widened... and you notice something else – you can see the blue sky above you... your branches have grown high enough, and now you can see the sunlight through the other trees...

You allow yourself to feel the warmth that the sun's rays are sending you... and the pleasant light that warms you... the warmth and the light reinforce your feeling that you are capable of growing in your own way... in the way that suits you and at your own pace...

And as time passes you continue to grow and develop... to grow in your own unique way... learning to progress more and more... you observe the other trees and you know that just like them you, too, can reach a great height and great strength... you have got patience to see it happen... the sapling you used to be has become a young tree... and continues to grow and become a large, impressive tree...

a tree that offers its shade and its fruit to others... a tree that assists saplings smaller than itself to grow... a tree that realizes its destiny...

And with this feeling of confidence in your unique way and in your ability to grow more and more... you are invited to begin to return to here, to this room... to feel your body... you take a deep breath... and another one... gently move your hands and your feet... and at your own pace open your eyes... and you return to normal awareness and normal wakefulness, to here and now.

36. Growing Towards the Light

37. The Tribe

Category:
Past

Who can benefit from this meditation?
People who seek their destiny, their role in society.

The Family

Everybody has a role in the family,
And its members are inter-dependent.
Check if your role – at home or at work –
Suits you, gives you a feeling of satisfaction.
If you feel frustrated in your present role,
Consider how you can find the best place for yourself.

Allow yourself to find a comfortable position... you will be able to feel your body on the chair or on the mattress... relax your muscles slightly... slowly start to feel comfortable... it is a time of rest for you... for your body... a time that allows the head to get rid of the thoughts and to loosen up... let your thoughts dissolve like bright clouds in the sky that move with the wind, dissolve and disappear... you will be able to hear voices from outside and the music playing here in the room... allow yourself to focus on my voice... and feel how you become more and more comfortable from minute to minute...

Imagine yourself to be part of an ancient tribe... it may be a nomadic tribe or may be a settled, agricultural tribe... and you are sitting on a hot summer evening at the campfire together with the other members of the tribe... around you are straw huts... and you can hear the voices of the members of the tribe talking among themselves... the sounds of adult conversation... the voices of children... mothers putting their children to sleep and singing lullabies... you can smell the smell of the campfire... the sky above you is strewn with stars, among them there is a full moon that shines a particularly strong light... the moon and the tribe remind you of something from your distant past... something ancient...

As you sit near the fire you are surrounded by your tribe... your family... the tribe is a community of people who have been together for years and know one another very well... and in the tribe everybody has a role... something he/she knows how to perform particularly well... a role that everybody else can trust will be played well... the tribe has a shaman and a midwife... there are hunters and there are gatherers... there are mothers with many children... there are story-tellers and wise old men and women who people come to for advice... and there are many other roles... and you also have a role in the tribe... your special role... you feel significant when you play your role...

I will now be quiet for about two minutes to allow you to connect to your ancient tribal role... you will be able to see yourself playing the role... to hear the reactions of the tribe members to your performance... to feel what you touch on in your work... or what tools you use... you will hear my voice again in about two minutes...

The ancient memory arose in you, and now you remember your role... after you experienced it, you can consider if it is also your role today or how the ancient role serves you in things that you do now... what has remained and what has changed... and perhaps today you do things completely differently...

You look at the moon rising in all its glory, round and white... and you feel it is looking at you with satisfaction, confident that you will find your destiny and bring your abilities to whatever society you find yourself in... the moon's confidence instills a sense of ability in you... of activity suited to you... breathe these good feelings deep inside yourself... the confidence in your ability...

And with this good feeling of confidence in your unique way and in your ability to grow more and more in this way... you are invited to return to here, to this room... to feel your body... you take a deep breath and slowly start to move your hands... and your feet... you take another breath... open your eyes at your own pace... you return to normal wakefulness and to full awareness... and to here and now.

37. The Tribe

38. The Thought Box

Category:
Solving Problems

Who can benefit from this meditation?
People who are interested in strengthening their ability to think positively.

Contradiction

*You are aware of contradictions
and conflicts in you.
Your head is constantly full
of contradictions.
This is the natural state
of conflicting forces.
Allow yourself to look at
things from above,
As if you are not involved
in them.
Try to understand
the situation and wait
till it passes.*

A llow yourself to find a comfortable position and close your eyes... perhaps you can hear voices outside or in the room... these voices help you to slowly focus your thoughts on all parts of your body... allow yourself to focus your attention on your head... to feel how comfortable the head is and how pleasant it feels... feel how it feels inside... it is pleasant to give your head attention... and now you can travel around your whole body with your attention... to your feet, slowly and gently... feel how this trip relaxes you more and more... when you get to your feet, you feel serene and calm... more and more...

Imagine yourself to be positioned next to a table on which is placed a magic box... it is a special and beautiful box... designed exactly in the style you like... allow yourself to look inside the box... perhaps it is new, perhaps old... you can feel it... get the feel of the material from which it is made... see the decorations on it... the stones of the drawings stuck on it, or any other thing... you can open it and look...

It is a very special box... it has various compartments... it can store thoughts... thoughts that you no longer need, that are superfluous for you, and you know you can manage without them in the near future... think about all the thoughts you would like to put into the box: perhaps your frequent criticism of yourself?... perhaps criticism of others?... perhaps contradictions that occur in your life?... perhaps deliberations that trouble you?... thoughts that prevent you from progressing?...

In one section of the box there are compartments in which you can also store thoughts that are troubling your mind at this moment... those that you want to keep for later... you can allow yourself to put the thoughts in the special compartment for this type of thoughts... knowing that when you need them they will be available for you... there is an additional part of the box that you do not open at the moment, though you know you will open it soon...

Allow yourself to store one thought after another in the box... it has endless space... all are preserved well... store every surplus thought that arises until you feel your head is free of thoughts... if you find it difficult to feel your head empty of thoughts, with your eyes closed, you will be able to focus your pupils on the top part of your nose for a few moments... this will help you to get rid of all thoughts...

And now allow yourself to imagine a ray of white light reaching your head, wrapping it in white light... slowly your head fills with this special light... light that is all calmness and quiet... you feel the light entering your head and filling it... the more it caresses your head, so the calmness inside your increases... you are filled with calmness and quiet... the light allows you to rest... rest you need badly... allow the light to move from your head to your neck... to your shoulders and shoulder blades... bring calmness to the places where in particular you often feel strain and tension... the light continues to fill your chest... the upper back... the stomach... the lower back... the whole upper part of your body is filled with a soft, pleasant light... and now the light also spreads to your hands... your pelvis... thighs... shins... and it goes on to fill your feet...

This light enables you to have total rest... relaxation... you feel your body fill with more and more calmness... and with the relaxation you can allow yourself to return to your thought box... after you have stored in it the criticism and the doubts... you can open the compartment you have not yet opened... the good thoughts compartment, and choose to take out from it positive thoughts... optimistic thoughts... encouraging thoughts, like "I can!"; "I am learning all the time and gradually succeeding more"; "I am able to realize my aspirations!"... there are a lot of good, affirming thoughts in the box that you can take with you... you can choose the exact thoughts you need... that boost your development process...

Allow the good thoughts to reach your head... you can choose what to think... it is possible to create reality using thoughts... and you create your reality made from good thoughts... that advance you...

The time has come to return... you can bring your thought box with you... or leave it where it is... it will always be there for you when you need it... feel how, as time passes, you use your ability to choose your thoughts more and more... from day to day you gain strength from the feeling that you can think only good thoughts... and create your reality...

And with this good feeling you begin to return to normal awareness here, to this room... you can move your hands and feet a little... move your body gently... move your head gently from side to side... take a deep breath... and another breath... slowly open your eyes and return at your pace to normal wakefulness and full awareness... and to here and now.

38. The Thought Box

39. Gliding in a Boat

Category:
Strengthening Resources

Who can benefit from this meditation?
People who encounter obstacles in their way and are interested in strengthening their ability to cope with them.

Obstacle

*Obstacles in our way are
connected to
Traces of our souls,
Or to a path we insist on
travelling.
Stop to check with yourself
what is preventing you from
advancing.
Allow yourself to consult
with others on the subject.*

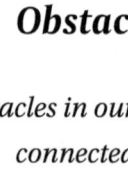

Allow yourself to find a comfortable position... and give yourself the possibility to relax... your body works hard and exerts itself the whole day and this is an opportunity to enable it to loosen up... and while you are comfortable on the mattress or on the chair, feel how all the places in your body where tension has built up, slowly relax, become calm... it is a pleasant feeling of release... allow yourself to breathe deeply and to take another breath and to let the air flow in your body... the air flows in the open places and sometimes it has difficulty flowing in blocked places... bring awareness to these places and allow them to open up... take another breath... and another... feel how the air brings serenity and calmness into the body, to each and every corner... and you connect more and more to the quiet in you...

Imagine yourself standing on the bank of a river... it is a beautiful, wide river... you can hear the sound of the raging water... and observe the colors of the water... green... blue... a smell of vitality rises in your nose... a boat is tied up next to the river bank... it is waiting for you... you get into the boat and embark on a trip on the river... there are soft cushions waiting for you in the boat that you can sit on... you very quickly understand how easy it is to steer the boat... the river flows gently... you are going to float with the current... you move on the waves and feel safe and protected... the swell of the water relaxes you... find it pleasant... you feel calmness spread around your body...

a pleasant calmness... the view around you is beautiful... the river is calm... and you are enjoying the trip...

You continue on until you see a large rock ahead of you... a rock that does not permit the boat to pass... you look at the rock and wonder, how will we get through?... it will be difficult to go around it because the opening is narrow and the rock is really blocking it... you are very keen to continue the journey that you started...

You stop the boat and wait... thinking what to do... you can only wait now... while you are waiting you notice that the river is starting to rise... the high tide is coming... you look around you and can see the water rising, the river is steadily filling up...

And like the river, you are also filled with optimism... the inner awareness that you have overcome many obstacles in your life and that you will overcome this one as well... you are filled with patience... patience allows you to wait, knowing that things will get sorted out soon... the water continues to rise, and as the river fills you feel you are filling with more patience... more and more... you feel you are also filling with belief... the belief that with optimism and patience you can certainly overcome this obstacle, too... you will be able to overcome difficulties... with belief you are capable of doing anything and succeeding...

You take a deep breath, fill your chest with fresh air and feel how you are filling up with optimism, patience and belief... the water goes on filling the river... and with it your boat also floats higher... you look at the rock again and discover that soon the water filling the river will cover it... then you will be able to get by the obstacle easily... on the sides, perhaps even in the middle...

A pleasant, relaxing feeling fills you... you understand that in times of difficulty it is sometimes preferable to wait patiently and with belief... and you start rowing the boat forward more and more... and behold – you have passed the obstacle so very easily that you are surprised...

the boat continues down the river... the water is calm and pleasant... you continue your journey... you know that every time you encounter an obstacle in your way you can wait... fill with optimism, patience and belief, and then get past the obstacle and continue your journey at your leisure... this knowledge fills you with happiness...

You have reached your destination, the end of your journey... you stop the boat, get out of it and tie it to the bank... you know that like the journey in the boat... your life is made up of sailing from place to place... objective to objective... and you can cope with the obstacles in your way...

And with this awareness you begin to return to here... take a deep breath... you embarked on a thought-provoking journey and now the time has arrived to return... it is a good feeling... special... and with this special feeling you are invited to begin to return slowly and gradually to here, to this room... you can move your hands and feet a little... take a deep breath... gently open your eyes and you slowly return... at your pace... to normal wakefulness... and to here and now.

39. Gliding in a Boat

40. The Water Pail

Category:
Solving Problems

Who can benefit from this meditation?
People who are interested to release certain things from their lives to clear space for new things.

Release

*Allow yourself to release
everything you
no longer need:
Anger, hostility or offence.
Release will enable you
to feel renewal,
And in this way you will be
able you to progress
and grow.*

Allow yourself to find a comfortable position... you will be able to feel your body on the chair or on the mattress... you close your eyes... and can feel the temperature of the room... you slowly begin to feel serenity and calmness... it is a time of rest for you... for your body that works the whole day... a time that allows the head to get rid of the thoughts and to loosen up... you are gradually filled with calmness and your body gets calmer and calmer... you will be able to hear voices from outside and here in the room... allow yourself to focus on my voice... and feel how you become more and more comfortable from minute to minute...

Imagine yourself to be standing in the middle of a big, expansive field... it is a beautiful field of flowers... the leaves are shades of light and dark green... among them flowers in an array of colors can be seen... you can hear the chirping of birds... and you feel a pleasant breeze blowing on your face and body... you feel safe and calm... you stand and look at the wide field... you bend down to examine a small flower of a color you like... you smell its scent... and when you straighten up you notice that a large gray cloud is covering the sky... it makes you very happy because you know it is about to rain... pleasant, refreshing rain, just as you like it... you can sense the pleasant smell preceding the rain and the smell of the earth yearning for water... you have an umbrella with you... and you can use it if you want to...

You feel the drops slowly beginning to fall on your face... one drop then another... you put out your hand and a drop lands on your finger... and as the drops continue to fall you feel more and more relaxed and calm... you lift your face upwards... your eyes are closed... you feel how the calmness in you increases with each drop... and there are a great many drops... you enjoy getting wet in the rain... the rainwater washes surplus emotions off you, perhaps anger, perhaps offence, perhaps hostility... they fall from you together with the drops of water... you feel secure and protected... and know that your good health can be preserved even now that you are wet...

You open your eyes and notice a large, lovely water pail... it is filling up with the wonderful drops of rain... you feel that every drop that collects in the pail is another idea germinating in your head... another new thought... or another amazing feeling you felt... slowly and gradually the pail fills with sparkling, clear drops of rain, and you feel more comfortable and calm...

The pail has completely filled with water and you notice the rain has stopped... the sun is again lighting the beautiful field... as well as the distant environment... you slowly start to get dry and you feel the sun warming your body... caressing it... this feeling fills you with happiness... and you are still happier when you look at your pail... it is full of sparkling drops of water... radiant... pure... that are your ideas, thoughts and emotions...

You take the pail with you and prepare to walk... you continue walking in the field while the sun dries your hair and your clothes... you feel full, like the pail, of love, calmness, quiet and confidence... you stride out holding the pail... at first the walk is pleasant... though after a short time you feel the pail is burdening you... it is heavy and the water is jumping around inside it with each step you take... you put the pail down and rest a bit... and again you pick it up and haul it along... you feel unsettled... and begin to search for a solution, how can you continue walking more easily?...

An idea arises... perhaps you can spill the contents of the pail on the ground and continue the walk without it... however, this thought raises doubts in you. How can you lose the sparkling drops... the ideas, the thoughts, the wonderful emotions you collected from the rain?... how can you relinquish all those wonderful things you collected and go on without them?... you continue to carry the pail and your whole body aches from the effort... you realize you cannot advance like this for long... carrying such a heavy load...

Finally, you place the bucket at the foot of a large apple tree... and then a new idea comes to you... you can water the tree with your good water... you know that all those drops will be preserved in the tree... in the trunk... between its branches... and leaves... and of course in the wonderful taste of the apples that grow on it... and if you feel you need your water, you will be able to find it easily in the tree... after watering the tree you continue walking, light and free, without any burden weighing you down... calm and serene... you also know new rain will fall soon... you will be able to fill your pail again with new ideas, thoughts and emotions... with sparkling drops... you will always be able to empty your pail and then fill it again... you will be able to preserve in you things that are important to you and release things you no longer need... and when a certain thing is released, space is vacated for something new... for clear, lovely, new drops of rain...

And with this feeling, you begin to make your way back... knowing that as time passes you can very easily release more things and receive new things... you can let go and know that all the resources you need remain at your disposal...

And with this knowledge and with the good feeling that accompanies it, you begin to return to normal awareness, to here, to this room... you can move your hands and feet a little... move your body gently... move your head gently from side to side... take a deep breath... and another breath... open your eyes and return at your pace to normal wakefulness and full awareness... to here and now.

40. The Water Pail

41. Between Tides

Category:
Solving Problems

Who can benefit from this meditation?
People whose are going through a difficult period in their lives and want to change the situation, to move from low tide to high tide.

Reduction

*This is a time of lessening
and reduction,
Ahead of the high tide.
It is a time for saving and a
simpler approach to life.
Be quiet, knowing
you can be economical,
With both fixed opinions
and wild emotions,
Ahead of future success.*

Allow yourself to find a comfortable position... you will be able to feel your body on the chair or on the mattress... relax your muscles slightly... slowly start to feel comfortable... it is a time of rest for you... for your body... a time that allows the head to get rid of the thoughts and to loosen up... let your thoughts dissolve like bright clouds in the sky that move with the wind, dissolve and disappear... you will be able to hear voices from outside and the music playing here in the room... allow yourself to focus on my voice... and feel how you become more and more comfortable from minute to minute...

You are standing at the side of a river on a warm, pleasant day... the sun's rays sparkle on the river... you look around you... everything around is painted in summer colors: brown... beige... yellow... orange... everything is dry... thirsty for water... you can hear the hushed sound of the wind... and you try to listen to the trickle of the water... yet you cannot hear the river water...

There is very little water in the river... the level is so low you can easily cross the river on foot... the river has dried up... it makes you sad... you feel that there is something dry, missing in your life as well... something that you would like to happen is not happening... it saddens you... like the river, you also feel you are thirsty... yearning for change... to quench your thirst...

You discover a corner where there is a little water and you begin to walk in the water... you wet your legs with the little water there is...

walking in the river bed calms you... you walk and feel the touch of the water on your legs... it caresses them... you feel the breeze blowing on your face... perhaps you do not know why you got into the river you are walking along... at the same time, there is something you want to clarify for yourself... to find why something in your life is now at a low point... just like this river...

You continue to walk towards the source of the river... where you notice something interesting: a large pile of stones has fallen from the bank into the river... these stones are blocking the way for the water... the water is dammed up and cannot flow further... you are happy to have found the place of difficulty and are sure you are now able to help the river refill with water... you feel the same will apply to your life... the moment you locate the difficulty you can begin to solve it...

You stop and begin to clear the stones from the river... it is hard work... some of the stones are heavy... and you have to climb on the bank to put them down... at the same time, you notice that a tiny opening has opened up, and a weak stream of water has begun to pass through it... you continue the hard work... the water gradually starts to flow down... the flow slowly increases... you know it is no longer necessary to move the stones because the water manages to pass easily... now you need only wait and see how the river fills again... you stand on the bank and feel the flow getting stronger...

Great happiness and satisfaction flood you. You managed to locate the difficulty and solve the problem... the river is flowing now and the level of the water is completely different from what it was at the start of your walk... you bend down and fill your hands with clean, cold water... drink your fill... you feel how your body fills up with good... pure... water... this water has healing properties – when it enters the body, it immediately creates a good... pleasant feeling...

You look at the river more and more... you understand that as time passes, your ability to find the resources to overcome any difficulty in your life will increase... that after every period of low tide comes a high tide... you can always return to the river and examine the flow of water that suits you... if the river is at low tide, you can restore the flow as you want with the aid of patience, willingness to work and resourcefulness, and the high tide is bound to come... and with this knowledge, you are, for the meantime, invited to depart from the river and to begin to make your way back to here, to this room...

This new knowledge fills you with joy and happiness like you experienced now... you begin to return here... you can move your hands and feet a little... move your body gently... move your head gently from side to side... take a deep breath... and another breath... slowly open your eyes and return at your pace to normal wakefulness and to full awareness... to here and now.

41. Between Tides

42. The Emotions Compass

Category:
Finding direction

Who can benefit from this meditation?
People who are interested to connect to their heart's compass and so find the right direction for themselves.

Benefit

*Allow yourself to benefit
from this time:
You will be able to avoid
doing things that do not
boost you,
(and may even harm you)
And begin to develop in
directions that are good for you.
Take an example from people
who function this way.*

Allow yourself to find a comfortable position... you will be able to feel your body on the chair or on the mattress... relax your muscles slightly... slowly start to feel comfortable... it is a time of rest for you... for your body... a time that allows the head to get rid of the thoughts and to loosen up... let your thoughts dissolve like bright clouds in the sky, that move with the wind, dissolve and disappear... you will be able to hear voices from outside and the music playing here in the room... allow yourself to focus on my voice... and feel how you become more and more comfortable from minute to minute...

Allow yourself to connect to your heart... try to sense it beating... to feel it... your heart is like a compass... a compass that directs you to places that suit you and are right for you...

As you start walking along a sandy path leading in the direction of the fields... allow the heart, your compass, to direct you... pay attention to what you see around you... what sounds you hear... what smells you can smell... perhaps there are thoughts going round your head... let them float in the air and let the wind carry them far from you...

You are walking along the sandy path and you have the opportunity to cut yourself off from all the everyday noises... to rest from all the expectations and demands and go your own way... purely as your heart guides you... your compass works through the emotions, and the path splits in different directions... you can try to walk in one direction and see what emotion arises... then perhaps you will want to try walking in another direction to check what emotion arises there...

Pay attention, maybe you are walking in a certain direction and the emotions that arise are of frustration... of helplessness... of tiredness... of impatience... this is a sign that the path you chose is not right for you... you can stop and examine this path... do you have to walk along it?... does it boost you in any way?... perhaps you would rather give it up in favor of another path?...

Again you feel your compass, your heart... you hear its beat... you trust it to lead you along the right path for you... and now you can ask the compass to suggest a completely different path – a path that arouses feelings of enthusiasm... excitement... expectation... hope... happiness and euphoria... perhaps worries will also arise, because it is a new, unfamiliar path... at the same time it will have something intriguing and challenging... something that will cause you to try to walk along it notwithstanding the worries... let yourself continue to walk and you will be able to constantly examine your emotions compass...

Maybe this is the first time you are using it... perhaps during your childhood you learned to behave only according to your mind... maybe it is difficult for you to follow your heart's compass... allow yourself to try out the experience and to test to what extent it is right for you... many people discover that their heart and their intuition allow them to be who they really are... to do what suits them... it helps them feel more satisfied with their lives...

All sorts of wonderful things await you on the new, unfamiliar path: perhaps there is a river you want to cross... perhaps you will discover a new world you don't yet know... maybe spectacular new scenery you have not yet discovered... perhaps new people you can meet... perhaps new opportunities to develop and grow... allow yourself to find a way to cross the river if your heart's compass leads you there...

I will now be quiet for about two minutes and I will allow you to use the compass to decide which way you should go... your compass will lead you on the best path for you; with it you can get to any place you want... you will hear my voice again in about two minutes...

You will now be able to find your way back from any place you get to... maybe you are returning along the same path you came on and maybe along a different path... perhaps you will go up a mountain on your way... or cross other rivers... perhaps you are marching across a plain... pay attention to your compass and you will be able to check what emotions crop up during every trial like this?

Your special heart's compass will enable you to live your life according to your heart... according to your intuition... to be connected to your center... to your path... to your choices... listening to the heart's compass can help us a lot with the choices we make in our lives... to help us remember ourselves and our needs... in a world where there are many demands and other people's needs, in a world that offers many and varied situations... you will always be able to find, with the help of the compass, your own way... allow yourself to make a sign to remind you to check what your heart wants at all times... maybe some thought... maybe some adventure or perhaps a place in your body that will remind you of the way of the heart...

And with this wonderful present, the ability to choose your path and to live according to your inclinations, your intuitions and your feelings... you are invited to begin to return slowly and gradually to here, to this room... and you begin to return to here... you can move your hands and feet a little... move your body gently... move your head gently from side to side... take a deep breath... and another breath... slowly open your eyes and return at your pace to normal wakefulness... to full awareness... and to here and now.

42. The Emotions Compass

43. The Crossroad

Category:
Finding direction

Who can benefit from this meditation?
People who are in the process of deciding and are struggling to choose.

Decisiveness

*This is the time to be decisive.
Weigh up the situation well
and check:
Does your decision-making
come from
Good and correct places for you?
Decisions made from the heart
will enable you,
To grow and to develop.*

Allow yourself to find a comfortable position... you will be able to feel your body on the chair or on the mattress... relax your muscles slightly... slowly start to feel comfortable... it is a time of rest for you... for your body... a time that allows the head to get rid of the thoughts and to loosen up... let your thoughts dissolve like bright clouds in the sky that move with the wind, dissolve and disappear... you will be able to hear voices from outside and the music playing here in the room... allow yourself to focus on my voice... and feel how you become more and more comfortable from minute to minute...

Imagine yourself to be walking in a dense forest on a pleasant winter day... the paths and the trees are wet after the rain... your feet make a slight rustle when they step on the leaves... you stride along looking at the tall trees... and the wet leaves hanging on them... you can smell the pleasant smell after the rain... and are enjoying the walk...

You want to use this walk to make a decision about your way forward... choosing a direction to continue walking in... you sense you will soon make a decision that excites you... as well as concerns you... though not worry - every decision you take will be the most fitting one you can make... and the best for you... you are striding along in the forest and you see a crossroad... until you reach the crossroad, on your way you will find a few items that will help you to decide what direction to take...

Pick up a stick from the ground... it is an exceptional stick... your intuition stick... it enables you to connect to your inner feelings... to connect to your heart... to decide according to your intuition what way suits you best...

You continue striding along the path and see large mushrooms growing on the trunk of a big tree... you look at the tall tree... how sturdy and strong it is – the mushroom can be fed by it and it does not disturb it at all... you pick a leaf from this big tree... this leaf will instill in you confidence in yourself and your ability to make the right decision... the leaf has been picked from a sturdy, strong tree... it will remind you to connect to the strength and confidence in you... to feel it in your body...

You see the crossroad from afar and know that you will soon be able to start making the decision... there is a beautiful, sparkling stone in a color you love, lying in the road... you pick up the stone and can feel its pleasant feel on your hand... it is a love stone... it will remind you that your choices are made out of love... out of self-love... from your desire to realize your dreams... and also out of love for people close to you... the stone symbolizes your love for yourself and for others...

Now you have the stick of intuition, the leaf of self-confidence and the stone of love, and you are marching with all of these towards the crossroad... it becomes clear to you that this is a extraordinary crossroad: a crossroad that allows you to try every one of the roads and to check if it suits you... only you know how many roads the paths splits into at the crossroad... only you know how you feel about each road... what the advantages and disadvantages are of each possible road... only you know what you can do on each of the roads...

Choose the first road that the stick of intuition indicates... and now you can go along it... allow yourself to take the first step... you have the ability to do so... walk and see how you feel about your choice... what can you see on the road you chose?... what noises can you hear?... what feelings arise in you?... you can continue and imagine what happens to you on this road... is it pleasant for you?... if you feel the need, you can return to the crossroad and try the second road the intuition stick points to...

Walk along the second road and see how you feel with this choice... what can you see on the road you have chosen?... what noises can you hear?... what feelings do you have?... you can continue and imagine what happens to you on this road... is it pleasant for you?... if you feel the need, you can return to the crossroad and try the next road the intuition stick points to...

And now you can allow yourself two minutes to think what road to choose... allow yourself to check where your intuition stick is pointing... you already have self-confidence, confident that you are capable of making the best decision... lovingly accept the choices you have made in your life until now, knowing that you can learn from every choice and develop... that every choice you make is right for you at the time you make it...

I will be quiet now for about two minutes, during which you can choose your way... your subconscious is wise enough to assist you with your choice or to advise you to wait... allow it to guide you... you will hear my voice again in about two minutes...

And now, you are fully satisfied in the knowledge that you have chosen... even if you chose to defer the decision, it is a choice... you feel excitement and happiness... you can slowly begin to return from the large forest... you can lock the intuition stick in your heart, the confidence leaf and the love stone, knowing that they will always help you throughout your life... you can come back to use them at any time...

And with this feeling of confidence in your unique way and in your ability to grow more and more... you are invited to return to here, to this room... to feel your body... take a deep breath... and another one... move your hands gently... and your feet... you open your eyes at your own pace... and return to normal wakefulness and normal awareness, to here and now.

43. The Crossroad

44. Weeding the Garden

Category:
Solving Problems

Who can benefit from this meditation?
People who need to be cleansed and freed of the old and are interested to grow the new in their lives.

Temptation

*Suddenly, temptation enters
the picture.
Is the temptation working for
your benefit?
Or is it perhaps returning you to
your weaknesses?
Indeed, it is easy to be tempted
into an inner temptation,
Though you can
say "no" to it.*

Close your eyes... find a comfortable position for your body... you will be able to hear the voices from outside and the voices from inside the room... you can enjoy the special music playing in the background... and focus on my voice... you are likely to be busy thinking... lot of things occupy you... allow yourself to relax a little from the thoughts in the knowledge that you can return to them later... try to focus your pupils in the direction of your nose – sometimes it helps the thoughts to rest... relax slowly and go into the quiet inside you... deep inside...

Imagine yourself standing in the heart of a vegetable garden... it is a fine garden in which the vegetables have been planted in rows... at the beginning of each row there is a sign with the name of the vegetable written on it... you look at the garden and see a row of carrots... a row of tomatoes... a row of radishes... and many more rows of vegetables...

Somebody has invested a lot in this garden... there is a low fence around it... and a large scarecrow stands in the middle... a nice garden, attractive... nevertheless, something about it disturbs you... something looks different from what you expect to see in a garden like this: it is full of weeds... as if they have forgotten to weed it... weeds grow between the vegetable plants... the weeds interfere with the growth of the plants... and they disturb your rest... for you it is a pity that a garden that could have been much nicer is full of weeds... you wonder what to do...

You bend down and begin to weed the garden... you feel the weeds as you pull them out of the ground and smell the good smell of the earth... some of the weeds come out easily, because the ground is slightly wet... and some you have to pull hard for their roots to come out of the earth... the sound of the pulling out of the weeds calms you a lot... there is a certain calm in working in a vegetable garden... when a pleasant sun is warming you from above... and you can hear the sound of the wind... and feeling of comfort fills you... it is pleasant for you to be in the vegetable garden... and you feel the weeding relaxes you...

Sometimes in life, too, it is difficult to see what is important because of weeds, all sorts of things that are unconnected... that are not really important to you... and you sense how the act of weeding also helps you to recognize what is important to you and what is not... what things are good and important to keep in your life... and what things you can throw out...

You uproot the weeds in one row after another, and discover more and more rows of vegetables that had difficulty growing... lots of weeds grew around them and prevented them from growing in the direction they wanted to... the weeds prevented their roots from getting to the source of water and food... and now that you are clearing the garden, you can see how easy and pleasant it is for the vegetables to grow... and how clean everything looks...

You are about to finish pulling out the weeds and can feel how, as time passes, you will be able to look at your life and know what is important for you to leave and what directions to take... and what you can give up... what plant will produce vegetables... and which and what are the weeds... that it is better to remove from the garden...

When you finish, you look at the garden for a minute... rows and rows of vegetables that will soon be ripe... you can see the scarecrow guarding the vegetables against the birds... and the fence protecting the saplings from other animals... soon it will be possible to pick the fresh vegetables and eat them... you feel you have done a right and important thing by weeding this garden...

You know you have the experience and the intelligence needed in your life to nurture the good, productive flowers and to relinquish the weeds that you don't need... you know how to protect your productive plants...

Now you notice that at the exit from the garden there is a sunshade that provide shade and a large inviting easy chair... there is a large glass of drink next to the chair... you allow yourself to sit down and take a rest from the work... you look with satisfaction at how nice the garden is now... you can see the vegetables growing in it clearly and easily... the cold drink quenches your thirst and you feel how every drop of it creates a pleasant feeling of satisfaction in you... great satisfaction fills your body... you can breathe in the satisfaction and enjoy it... and with the feeling of satisfaction from the weeding in the garden and the good rest that followed it, you slowly begin to return to here, to this room... to your body, to this special day...

And with the knowledge and these new insights, you can move your hands and feet a little... move your body gently... move your head gently from side to side... take a deep breath... and another breath... slowly open your eyes... and return at your pace to normal wakefulness... to full awareness... to here and now.

44. Weeding the Garden

45. The Success Ball

Category:
Past

Who can benefit from this meditation?
People who are interested to remember the successes
in their lives, and to draw strength from them
to continue and succeed.

Gathering

*This is the time to gather yourself
and focus inward.
Self-focus will enable you to
be part of social activity,
By knowing what
is good for you,
And what is right for you.
Inward focusing will enhance,
The social gathering
required now.*

Allow yourself to find a comfortable position... you will be able to feel your body on the chair or on the mattress... relax your muscles slightly... slowly start to feel comfortable... it is a time of rest for you... for your body... a time that allows the head to get rid of the thoughts and to loosen up... let your thoughts dissolve like bright clouds in the sky that move with the wind, dissolve and disappear... you will be able to hear voices from outside and the music playing here in the room... allow yourself to focus on my voice... and feel how you become more and more comfortable from minute to minute...

Today you are invited to a ball... an enormous ball at the king's palace... you get dressed in special clothes suited to a ball... it is a special ball... it is intended specially for you... it is your success ball... they will all be there... all the successes you remember and the ones you have forgotten...

You examine your appearance before setting off... your clothes are beautiful and elegant... your reflection in the mirror, wearing the beautiful clothes, calms you... makes you comfortable in expectation of what lies ahead... you are also excited ahead of the royal ball... you feel the clothes... the feel of the material is very pleasant... hark, you hear the sound of the carriage approaching... you go outside and walk towards it...

You climb into the carriage... the carriage boy takes you... the carriage rocks like a crib... gently and pleasantly... you sit comfortably... look out of the window... hear the horse's steps... and the boy's cries... the journey relaxes you...

You reach the ancient, beautiful, tall palace... the carriage boy helps you descend and leads you to the entrance... at the entrance your name is called out and the king himself greets you and invites you in... he is wearing gilded clothes and has a crown studded with precious stones on his head... he tells you that all your successes have already arrived... all the invitees are sitting around the table expecting you...

You enter a spacious hall... chandeliers hang from above and cast light everywhere... there is a large table around which there are a great many people... these are your successes... you can see successes that you have long forgotten: the first time you started crawling... the first step you took... the first word you said... and newer successes as well... successes at work... successes in the family...

There are a great many successes there... and they are all sitting and smiling at you... you are surprised by how many successes you have totally forgotten... like the day you read your first word in a book... like the successful exam... like the praise you received...

You sit down and smile at those sitting around the table... all your successes come one at a time and embrace you warmly... you remember the unique story of each and every one... how happy you were about it then... how proud you were... how quickly you forgot them... how good it is to recall... you listen to the successes and get the messages they are sending you... messages of success are reaffirming... I will now be quiet for about two minutes... you can look around you and be reminded of more and more successes in your life... big as well as small... listen to the successes... to their messages to you... you will hear my voice again in about two minutes...

And you are filled with a good feeling of ability... a feeling of capability... all the many successes in the room are yours... they are wonderful... you can hear their pleasant voice... you remember the happy moments... and realize there are too many to count...

Time has passed and it is time to leave... the king starts leading you to your carriage... he invites you to come again to his palace to meet your successes whenever you want, if you feel the need...

You reach the exit where the carriage boy is waiting for you... you sit down in the carriage... on the way back you feel lighter... happier... and with these feelings you return to your house...

And with this good, encouraging feeling, you are invited to begin to return slowly and gradually to here, to this room... you begin to return here... you can move your hands and feet a little... move your body gently... move your head gently from side to side... take a deep breath... and another breath... slowly open your eyes and return at your pace to normal wakefulness... to full awareness... and to here and now.

45. The Success Ball

46. A Message from Childhood

Category:
Past

Who can benefit from this meditation?
People who want to remember pleasant things from their childhood.

Ascent

*You can now achieve
anything you need.
Until now you have invested
work and effort,
And very soon great success
will greet you.
Investing in small things will
lead you to great success.
Keep on going.*

Allow yourself to rest a little... ease off from everyday matters... find a comfortable position... close your eyes and allow them to rest from all visions... and let your ears rest from the many voices and focus on my voice... feel the chair or the mattress you are sitting or lying on... all your senses are resting now... relaxing more and more... your brain which is responsible for thoughts is also resting... the heart, responsible for feelings, rests... you feel calmer and calmer... and are ready to embark on a journey... a journey of the imagination... a journey open to everything... a journey on which anything can happen... and everything is safe and protected... allow yourself to embark on this special journey... wonderful and magical... a journey totally for the benefit of your personal development...

Imagine yourself in an old house... it is an ancient house and something about it attracts you... it has ancient furniture and many rooms... it has a large staircase going down to a mysterious basement... you are very curious to know what is in this basement... and decide to go down the stairs... ancient stone stairs around which is an ancient, decorated banister... the stairs are lit by a soft, gentle light...

You go down the stairs and feel pleasantly relaxed... as you descend, you feel more and more calm... there is something pleasant about the smell hovering over the stairs... you can hear the sound of your steps as you descend... you get more and more relaxed... and reach the ancient basement... it is also lit by a soft light... and you discover that there are old books and objects in it... the objects are well kept... they are objects you had when you were little... and when you grew up they were put and they waited for you...

You will be able to find books that you read during your childhood and be reminded of them... games and toys you had... you sense there is an important message hidden in these objects... a message from the girl or boy you used to be, and it is important to remember him/her now, because he/she can help you...

You happily engage with your things... you are alone in the room with objects from your childhood... you let yourself touch... feel... play... actually feel like a little child... like the child you were, when you played... I will be quiet for about two minutes to allow you to play... to enjoy yourself... to remember... you will hear my voice in two minutes...

A pleasant feeling accompanies you when you remember your toys and books... a childhood song plays in the background... you remember that there were lots of happy moments in your childhood, forgotten a bit... you are happy to remember them again... and you begin to understand the message that will help you with something that preoccupies you at the moment... something that the child inside you wants to remind you of... listen to the message (wait a moment)...

And after you have received the message, you cast another glance at the objects from your childhood... at your memories... you feel the warmth that has filled you... the meeting with the things from your childhood made you very excited and happy... you begin to ascend the stairs... and you feel you are ascending lightly... as if you are hovering above the stairs and they are taking you higher and higher... higher than the floor of the house... as if the stairs are lifting your forward... taking you to another place... a place you aspire to... a place you want to get to...

You understand that when you are attentive to the message from the child inside you, it is easy for you to progress... to go higher and higher... and even if his/her messages are bleak sometimes... they enable you to understand yourself better... and you advance and go higher and higher... you are moving ahead towards achieving your goals... slowly and gradually you establish yourself in a place that suits you best... and continue to feel light and comfortable... happily looking ahead...

And with this comforting expectation and with the insights you gained, you can begin to return to here and now, to this room... you can move your hands and feet a little... move your body gently... move your head gently from side to side... take a deep breath... and another breath... slowly open your eyes and return at your pace to normal wakefulness... to full awareness... and to here and now.

46. A Message from Childhood

47. Connecting to the Light

Category:
Strengthening Resources

Who can benefit from this meditation?
People who are in difficulty and need resources to cope.

Hardship

*Like everything in nature,
There are times of multiple difficulties.
This is the time
to be helped by,
Your inner resources
To be optimistic and confident,
To focus on realizing
your dreams,
Notwithstanding
the difficulties.*

Allow yourself to find a comfortable position... grant yourself the possibility to rest... your body works and exerts itself throughout the day and this is an opportunity to relax a little... once you are comfortable on the chair or on the mattress, feel how all the places in your body in which tension has built up slowly begin to relax... it is a pleasant feeling of release... let yourself breathe deeply, and another breath, and let the air flow in your body... the air flows through the open places and sometimes has difficulty flowing in the blocked places... send awareness to these places and allow them to open... take another breath... and another... feel how the air brings calmness and serenity into your body, to each and every corner... and you connect more and more to the quiet in you...

Imagine yourself as a tree living in a forest... a small, green tree... in a forest in which many trees are growing... you can see a clump of trees around you... you can feel the contact of the branches of the trees near you... the forest is quiet and pleasant... birds fly above you... you can hear their pleasant twittering... and feel the wind of a winter day... the wind brings a pleasant fragrance of fresh grass... you are among a great many trees... your roots are planted in the ground... your top is high... you feel a strong urge to grow... to develop... to reach your objective... to realize your dreams...

At the same time, when you try to grow and develop you encounter a difficulty... the trees around you are so dense that you have no room to develop... every attempt you make to grow meets resistance... the other trees do not mean to make things difficult for you – they also want to grow, and that is how the density is created...

Your branches try to leap upwards and advance, though they hit the branches of neighboring trees... who want to do the same... you are in great difficulty... it sometimes seems that the tall trees are shading you... perhaps looking down on you...

Your desire to grow is strong and you look up... you see the clear sky and the warm rays of the sun... you decide to focus on the light... to focus on the pleasant sunshine... when you focus on the sun you feel how the strong light pulls you up and up, and slowly and gradually space opens up for your personal growth... your branches begin to climb... your trunk strengthens... you are filled with joy because you discover that as you advance in the sunlight, you can advance and move upwards...

Allow the sunlight to light up your progress, warm you and fill you with growth resources... the light fills you completely with belief in your ability... you remember past incidents when you succeeded to overcome difficulties and obstacles and you feel you are gaining strength... able to cope with any situation, as you coped in the past... you are filled with the light of belief in your ability...

The sunlight fills you with determination... strengthens your ability to withstand any situation and to keep going... your will is very strong and it enables you to continue... feel your determination to achieve your goals and let your whole body fill with it...

Allow yourself to fill with self-acceptance as well... accept yourself as you are... be forgiving towards yourself... if you can accept yourself as you are, you will be able to cope with any situation successfully... you will feel more satisfied... knowing that at each stage you did the best you could at that time...

Allow the sunshine to fill you with this belief... that your determination and your ability to accept yourself as you are... breathe this ability into yourself... fill your whole body with the warm, pleasant light that allows you to grow...

Now that you feel your treetop is almost touching the sun... and the sun's rays are warming you... you can remember the smile you started off with... when you were a very small tree and you struggled to advance in the dense forest... how much you have grown since then and been filled with wonderful powers... nowadays you can help the small trees in the forest to advance and grow... as time goes on, you use your strength to help others... you use all the things you learned to help others on their way...

And the more you help others... so you gain strength... your leaves grow... your branches grow, and your trunk broadens, and stabilizes...

And with this welcome news and with the generosity you can allow yourself and show to others, you begin to return here, to this room... take a deep breath... you embarked on a thought-provoking journey and now the time has arrived to return... it is a good feeling... special... and with this feeling you are invited to begin to return slowly and gradually to here, to this room... you can move your hands and feet a little... take a deep breath, gently open your eyes... and you return slowly... at your own pace... to normal wakefulness... and to here and now.

47. Connecting to the Light

48. The Well

Category:
Strengthening resources

Who can benefit from this meditation?
People who are interested in connecting to their source.

The Source

*The source of the water,
the well,
Is located in the depths
of your soul,
And it is the source of your desires
and needs.
In order to realize yourself,
Allow yourself to return
to the source.*

Allow yourself to find a comfortable position... grant yourself the possibility to rest... your body works and exerts itself throughout the day and this is an opportunity to relax a little... once you are comfortable on the chair or on the mattress, feel how all the places in your body in which tension has built up slowly begin to relax... it is a pleasant feeling of release... let yourself breathe deeply, and another breath, and let the air flow in your body... the air flows through the open places and sometimes has difficulty flowing in the blocked places... send awareness to these places and allow them to open... take another breath... and another... feel how the air brings calmness and serenity into your body, to each and every corner... and you connect more and more to the quiet in you...

Imagine yourself standing in the center of a small village... it is an ancient village... where everything happens just as it did once... a long time ago... you look around you and see ancient houses... alleyways... you can hear the people's voices... the sound of conversation... the sound of laughter... the sound of traders offering their wares... something in this village attracts you... you can smell the fragrance of cooking and you feel thirsty... you want to drink water...

There is a well in the heart of the village... you walk towards it... it is an ancient well, built of stone... it is located in the middle of a large, beautiful square... there is a pail on the side of the well that can be lowered to draw water... you approach the well and take the pail... you lower it into the depths of the well... as the pail goes down deeper... so your serenity deepens... you become more and more calm and serene...

The water in the well is pure and good... you will soon be able to sip it... the pail has reached the water and it fills up... you begin to turn the special handle in order to bring it up... slowly, slowly... the pail is heavy and full to the brim... you struggle to bring it up... you feel the effort in your muscles... and you persevere... you very much want to taste the cold water... one more turn... and the pail has reached the top...

And you pour a little water for yourself into a glass standing near the well... and you drink your fill from it... the water is pure and clear... very tasty... you sip it and feel how it quenches every cell in your body... the water is so good...

Like this well, your source is there, deep in your heart... it is a place from which you can draw the right water to satisfy you... the source enables you to know what is right for you... what you really want... what your needs are... what insights you can dredge up... to find your inner truth...

Your inner source has tremendous strength... it has abilities that will boost you in anything you want to do... you will always be able to draw from the source, from your well, self confidence... belief... self-guidance... the source, your well, is the inner place from which you can draw what is correct and real for you... allow yourself to go deep in order to discover your source... to feel when you are functioning from within it...

I will now be quiet for two minutes to allow you to go down into the depths of your heart... to the well, to the source, and get answers to your questions... you can actually send down a pail on a rope to reach the depths of your heart and receive a message regarding the way ahead... you will hear my voice again in two minutes...

And after you have received the message... you experience a pleasant sensation... you consider the message and realize you have a wonderful source... when you draw from the well, from your source, you are fed by the right places for you... and you feel good with yourself...

You slowly leave the well in the heart of the village and go on your way, knowing that you can always return and draw nourishing water from it... you will always be able to receive nourishing and direction from your well... as time passes you will feel how to reach your inner well more easily... you will be able to be more precise about your feelings... in fulfilling and feeding your needs...

And with these beneficial feelings, you begin to make your way back from the ancient village to here, to this room... slowly and gradually you begin to return to here... you can move your hands and feet a little... move your body gently... move your head gently from side to side... take a deep breath... and another breath... slowly open your eyes... and return at your pace to normal wakefulness and to full awareness... and to here and now.

48. The Well

49. The Bus of the Future

Category:
Future

Who can benefit from this meditation?
People who are interested in using the tools they have collected along the way and look to the future.

Change

*Environmental forces
are leading you,
To a change you really need.
Now you can adopt a new
standpoint,
And change
what needs changing.
If you look at the change
positively,
Others will also be able to
accept it more easily.*

Allow yourself to close your eyes and find a comfortable position... feel the contact of your body with the chair or the mattress... and the temperature of the room... perhaps you can hear voices from outside and voices and sounds in the room... allow yourself to focus on my voice and slowly connect to a quiet place in you... to the quiet in you... today you are going to embark on an extraordinary journey... and perhaps you are a little excited at the prospect... allow yourself to take a deep breath and to fill yourself with serenity, knowing that this journey will reach just the right places for you... feel how you rest and relax your muscles... more and more...

Imagine you are waiting at a bus stop... today you are going on an important journey... the thought of the journey that awaits you fills you with calmness and expectation... you really like travelling on the old, special bus... here it comes and it stops near you... the door opens and you climb aboard... the driver gets off and vacates his place for you... from now on you are the driver of the bus...

Before you sit down on the driver's seat you look carefully at the bus... it has a lot of resources and abilities... it looks to you like a sort of long tool box... there is something you have learned in life on each bench... insight... ability... good quality... inner resource... and all of them join you on your journey to the future...

You sit down... the steering wheel is in your hands... and you can navigate your way... the area is familiar though it is a new road and you are travelling along it for the first time... you know that there is a map in the bus that will help you to find your way...

Today you are travelling towards your future... you choose where and when to stop... perhaps in a year's time... in two years or five or ten year's time?... there, at the destination, a man or woman is waiting for you, like you... from the future... you may notice that your future image is a little different from you... maybe the hairstyle... perhaps the figure... maybe the clothes...

You stop at the stop and get off... your future image welcomes you... you like it... it has something serene about it that creates a pleasant ambience... it is holding a tool box like the one you have in the bus... and you understand that it has acquired additional tools to help it cope with the things that you are currently pondering about... today you can sit and talk with your future image, and it will show you its life as it is today, namely, in your future...

You have sat down in a pleasant spot and it offers you a photograph album... soon it will show you the things it has undergone since it was you, until today... how it resolved the deliberations, the problems, how it coped with the things you are contending with today...

The album looks nice and new... the photos are black and white and there is something special about them... they are moving, like images on television... here you are like you are today, and here are the photos that tell what has happened in the years that have passed since then... I will now be quiet for three minutes to allow you to look at the photos...

You have finished looking at the photos and hearing the fascinating stories from your future image... you understand a few new things... it becomes clearer and clearer to you how it coped with situations, what it did and where it is now... it offers you a folded page with a message for you written on it... you open the paper and read the message... perhaps you can hear it... it really excites you... (wait a moment).

You part company in a way that suits you, whether a hug, a caress or another way... knowing that you can always meet up again, with your future image... you return to the bus that is waiting for you at the stop... you add the card to your tool box in the bus and begin to drive back... to the stop you set out from... you feel that from now, as time passes, you will be able to succeed more and more in what you do, and some important things have become clearer...

And with this sensation you return to the stop and return the bus to the driver... the driver invites you to return to the stop and go on other journeys whenever it takes your fancy... he gives you your tool box... all the things your brought with you and all the things you added are in the box...

And from the stop you slowly return to this room... to a state of normal wakefulness and normal awareness... at a pace that suits you, allow yourself to feel your body again... and to open your eyes.

49. The Bus of the Future

50. The Plate of Stones

Category:
Future

Who can benefit from this meditation?
People who want to create a clear scale of values in their lives in order to live in harmony.

Cosmic order

It is a wonderful time:
Your needs and the
environment's
Are in harmony and are
coordinated.
You can allow yourself to grow,
And to promote initiatives
and ideas.
Your potential
is reaching its peak.
Prosperity and blessing
will reign in your
abode.

Allow yourself to find a comfortable position... close your eyes... pay attention to the sounds outside and to those you can hear in the room... allow the sounds to help you focus your attention on my voice... today you are embarking on a journey of growth and learning... and perhaps you are excited ahead of the journey... your subconscious is very wise and takes care of you, so you can loosen up knowing that it is doing its job in the best possible way... allow yourself to slowly and gradually get into a state of relaxation and calmness... to rest a little from everyday thoughts and activity and simply breathe deep... and listen...

Imagine yourself sitting near a large window in an pleasant room... the sun's warm rays come from outside to light up and caress the room... the scene creates a sense of serenity in you... on the window sill there is a large glass plate with lots of precious stones on it... each stone has its own shape and color... every stone is exceptional... you look at the stones... feel them... some feel smooth and nice... some are jagged and sharp... among them there are stones whose color you like a lot, and some stones attract you less...

Your life also looks like this plate of stones sometimes... it contains lots of events... thoughts... lots of things... and at times you just want some time to sit and think what is important and what is not so important... what is really significant for you and what things can you give up or pay less attention to... today you can create order in your life by using the plate of stones... to decide what is most important and what can wait till later... to create a cosmic circle of you values...

You remove all the stones from the plate and gently place them on the window sill... one stone after the other... you can see how the sun's rays sparkle in and through the stones... you are filled with serenity and calmness... you have emptied the plate and it now sparkles... you take a deep breath and begin to arrange the stones in circles, from the center to the edge of the plate... perhaps you are deliberating where to put each stone... allow yourself to deliberate, so that you can reach the best decision... your subconscious is wise and it will help you decide easily...

Soon the stone most important to you will be positioned at the center... perhaps it is the stone of love... perhaps the stone of family... perhaps the stone of success or career... take a moment to choose which stone is most important to you at this time... it is likely to change in the future... in the meantime allow yourself to find what is most important to you at this stage of your life (wait a moment)...

Now take the stone you have chosen and feel it... look at its color and its reflectivity... and place it at the center of the plate... this stone is the heart, the center, the thing that is more important to you than anything else...

Around this stone you can begin to arrange the rest of the stones according to the importance of things in your life... take one stone at a time, consider what the stone represents for you and place it on the plate according to its level of importance... stones that are very important will be placed around the central stone and stones that are less important will be placed further out... in this way, circle upon circle of stones will be created, from the most important to the less important... I will now be quiet for a minute to allow you to arrange the plate in the way that suits you best... you will hear my voice in one minute...

You look at the arranged plate... how beautiful and glittering it is... every stone has found its place... as time passes you will feel how the array of stones and its order of importance guide you... for every decision in your life you will be able to be reminded what is most important to you and behave accordingly... the stones sparkle at you in order and in harmony... the sight is magical... and from the order you now have in your life you can advance and grow in directions you want... to advance towards your goals... according to your set of values and credo...

And with this wonderful present, with the ability to map your priorities in life... knowing what is more and what is less important... to live according to your heart's desire... you are invited to begin to return slowly and gradually to here, to this room... and you begin to return here... you can move your hands and feet a little... move your body gently... move your head gently from side to side... take a deep breath... and another breath... slowly open your eyes and return at your pace to normal wakefulness... to full awareness... and to here and now.

50. The Plate of Stones

51. The Calm after the Storm

Category:
Solving Problems

Who can benefit from this meditation?
People who have undergone a significant change or been through a difficult period and are now beginning a new period.

Turbulence

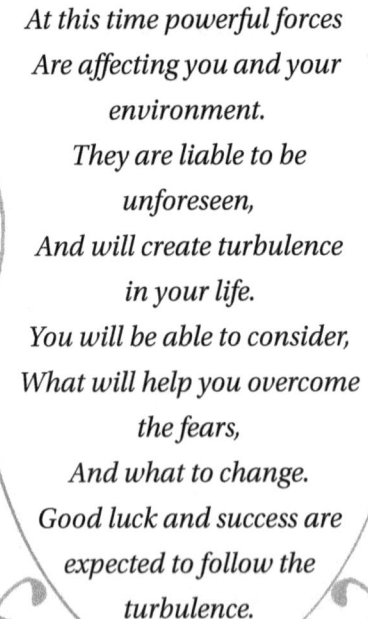

At this time powerful forces
Are affecting you and your environment.
They are liable to be unforeseen,
And will create turbulence in your life.
You will be able to consider,
What will help you overcome the fears,
And what to change.
Good luck and success are expected to follow the turbulence.

Allow yourself to find a comfortable position... you will be able to feel your body on the chair or on the mattress... relax your muscles slightly... slowly start to feel comfortable... it is a time of rest for you... for your body... a time that allows the head to get rid of the thoughts and to loosen up... let your thoughts dissolve like bright clouds in the sky that move with the wind, dissolve and disappear... you will be able to hear voices from outside and the music playing here in the room... allow yourself to focus on my voice... and feel how you become more and more comfortable from minute to minute...

Imagine yourself on a large covered balcony... in a charming cabin overlooking a forest... you are sitting in an armchair and looking ahead... far away you see the trees, the sky and rain clouds... you look at the trees in the forest... and allow yourself to relax in this magical winter atmosphere... you notice the first drops of rain on the ground...

It starts to rain... slowly the drops increase... and become heavy rain... the rain wets the ground... you can hear the sound of the falling rain... and the drops... you can smell the fragrance of the wet earth... the rain gets heavier and heavier... at first it calms you... afterwards, as it gets heavier and heavier, it calms you less...

You see lightning... a few seconds later... you hear the sound of thunder rumbling... the rain comes and gets heavier... the sky darkens... clouds cover it... a storm has arrived... the drops of water reach you... and wet you... then there is another flash of lightning... it lights up the forest... and is followed by thunder... and then darkness again... and it is cold... the strong wind blows leaves and branches all over...

This storm reminds you of the storms in your life... moments of fear... during which your confidence is undermined... and things seem not to be in their normal place... when the feeling is that the wind has blown everything away in a storm... forcefully... and suddenly reality changes... and it takes time to get used to it...

The storm outside continues to rage around you... perhaps you are a little scared and decide to go inside, into the protected cabin... inside you can still hear the noises from outside... sometimes the noise sounds worse than it really is... sometimes storms create a lot of noise... though when they subside everything goes back safely to its place... the noise is frightening, though afterwards the calmness returns... some storms create change in life... that create a new situation... and you wonder what type of storm is occurring now... sometimes the storm going on in our head is bigger than the one outside... and sometimes we create the storm ourselves...

And slowly the storm subsides... the sound of the thunder moves further away... no more lightning is to be seen... the rain gradually stops... and the sky clears... you can go outside and see what has changed... maybe the wind has blown leaves around and broken trees... animals that went into hiding come out slowly to look for food... flowers that closed in the downpour reopen slowly... you can see how the world has calmed down, and with it you also relax more and more... you realize that the storm has passed and that you can also get through storms and be protected...

The sun's rays penetrate the clouds and send light to the ground... it is a beautiful sight... to see how the light looks for a way and returns... and how the quiet calms everything... the calm after the storm... you notice the strong trees that withstood the storm... there are some strong trees that remain upright and survive the storm, and others bend and the storm passes over them and does not damage them... each tree in its own way... you remember that you were able to endure the storms that occurred in your life... and finally the calmness arrived... and the light returned... and balance returned to life...

The sun's rays are warm and pleasant... and you also feel quiet and relaxed... you know that even if there is another storm you will be safe and protected... you will be able to cope with it safely... in life there are periods of calm... periods of storms... calm periods... stormy periods... we are able to choose how to cope with the difficulties... and we have lots of resources to do this... allow yourself to be calm and serene and to enjoy the quiet now...

And with a feeling of confidence in your ability to experience storms, to survive them in your particular way... you are invited to begin to return to here, to this room... to feel your body... you take a deep breath... and another one... gently move your hands... and feet... open your eyes at your own pace... and return to normal wakefulness... to full awareness, to here and now.

51. The Calm after the Storm

52. The Mountain

Category:
Strengthening resources

Who can benefit from this meditation?
People who are interested in looking at their lives, and then doing a soul-search of the past, the present and the future.

Stopping

*It is time to let go.
You are invited to go inside,
Into the depths of your soul,
And allow yourself
to re-orientate.
Allow your thoughts to enter
a quiet sleep,
And rise above what is
going on around you.*

Allow yourself to find a comfortable position and close your eyes... perhaps you can hear sounds outside or from inside the room... these sounds help you to focus your thoughts slowly on all parts of your body... allow yourself to focus your attention on your head... feel how comfortable and pleasant your head feels... sense how it feels from inside... it is pleasant to pay attention to the head... and now you can wander with your attention around your whole body... down to your feet, slowly, slowly and gently... feel how this stroll calms you more and more... and when you reach your feet, you feel calm and serene... more and more...

Imagine yourself sitting comfortably on a large lawn... it is a pleasant winter day... the sun's rays emerge from behind the clouds and gently warm your body... you can find a comfortable position on the expanse of the lawn and hear the quiet around you... you are alone and, at the same time, feel safe and calm...

There is a high mountain opposite you... an impressive mountain... you look at the mountain... at its height... at its firm stance... its stability... its might... this mountain attracts your attention... perhaps part of the mountain is covered by trees... and part is barren, covered with stones and earth... perhaps it is a mountain whose peak is snow-covered... you can imagine how your mountain looks, to suit you...

The mountain instills serenity and calmness in you... something in it relaxes you... allows you to go inside yourself... to a place of quiet...

to a place of rest and calmness... the mountain stands where it is... quietly... the mountain allows itself quiet contemplation...

You notice that on the mountain opposite you there is a mirror... an extraordinary mirror... a mirror in which your image is reflected... an image of you at a good time in your life... a period in your life during which you were happy... you look at yourself as you were then... you see your body... your look and expression... you see how you move... you see what was happening at that time...

I will now be quiet for about two minutes to allow you to look at yourself at that happy period in your life... you will hear my voice again in about two minutes...

Looking at yourself at that time makes you happy... allows you to remember... and you bid farewell to your image from then... the mirror is about to change its face... now your present image is seen in the mirror on the mountain... you see yourself today, and this allows you to detect what has changed... what could you have brought from that period into your life today?... you look... the mountain allows you the calmness to examine this... what things you summon into your life nowadays... (wait half a minute).

And again the mirror changes... and you see your image of two year's time... looking at you... this image has already dealt with the things you are dealing with today... it has already learned a thing or two, and wants to share with you what it discovered... the way of dealing it chose... you look at it and hear its voice... I will now be quiet for one minute to allow you to hear its message... you will hear my voice again in one minute...

The time has come to depart from your future image in the mirror... you are happy to have met it... you got an important message from it... you know you can come back and talk to it when you need it again... you notice that all along there has been silence on the mountain... it is still standing there firm and stable... quiet... silent... you allow yourself to feel like the mountain... silent and serene... stable and comfortable... receiving insights from your past... and from your future... insights that allow you to find a balance and calmness in your life...

And with this understanding, you begin to return here... you take a deep breath... you have embarked on a thought-provoking journey and now the time has arrived to return... it is a good feeling... special... and with this special feeling you are invited to begin to return, slowly and gradually, to here, to this room... you can move your hands and feet a little... take a deep breath... and another breath... gently open your eyes... and return slowly... at your pace to... to normal awareness... to here and now.

52. The Mountain

53. Born Again

Category:
Strengthening resources

Who can benefit from this meditation?
People who feel they want to change, develop, grow and reveal themselves.

Development

*Things are developing very
slowly and gradually
at the moment,
Connecting to yourself
and to your guiding values,
Can help you to develop in a
way that suits you.
Slow development will
bear fruit when the time
arrives.*

Allow yourself to find a comfortable position and close your eyes... perhaps you can hear sounds outside or from inside the room... these sounds help you to focus your thoughts slowly on all parts of your body... allow yourself to focus your attention on your head... feel how comfortable and pleasant your head feels... sense how it feels from inside... it is pleasant to pay attention to the head... and now you can wander with your attention around your whole body... down to your feet, slowly, slowly and gently... feel how this stroll calms you more and more... and when you reach your feet, you feel calm and serene... more and more...

Imagine yourself as a fetus a few weeks old living in the womb... in the warm, pleasant fluid... you feel the motion of the fluid... you feel your mother's movements...

You are still very small... you have a lot of room in the tummy... among the gurgling sounds of the fluid you also gradually begin to hear sounds from outside... you develop slowly... very easily... in harmony and coordinated with the natural processes...

Through the umbilical cord connected to your mother you get all the things you need... your mother feeds you well... and it contributes to your sound and healthy development... you continue to float in the fluid... calm and comfortable... you simply rest... you know you are receiving all you need at all times... you grow and gain strength naturally all the time...

Your facial features take shape... as well as your hands and feet... your tiny fingers are visible... every day your fetal body grows and grows... your mind develops... your heart goes on beating... you grow and grow... getting stronger...

Now you can move your arms and legs... and even suck your finger... from day to day you grow and become more and more similar to the infant we all know... you develop gradually... you can turn over from side to side... you feel when your mother moves and like the motion of her body... when your mother rests you begin to move... jump and turn over...

You grow so much that there is less and less room in mother's tummy... it has got a bit crowded for you... and squashed... something in you likes very much being in the tummy... enjoying the softness and the comfort... however, something in you wants to leave... to find a bigger space... perhaps with more light... where you can move...

And then you begin to push downwards with your head... you want to get out... you know your mother is mindful of you and she knows you want to get out into the world... you feel mother is ready to help you... at the same time, you know you will have to do it by yourself...

You continue to push and press and you pass through a canal... the canal is narrow and dark and it is a bit frightening... you battle... certain that soon you will be out of it and you will see strong, bright light... soon you will get out and you will be able to see the faces of the people who love you outside... the world outside intrigues you and you want to see it...

Suddenly you feel you have to get through the canal, and your head is out... and your body follows... you get out... you give a short cry of departure from the womb... a pleasant light meets your eyes... you are embraced by your mother's arms... she looks at you excitedly... slowly and gradually you matured and came out, to the light... to life... to everything that waits for you there outside...

As time passes you will continue to grow and develop in the big world... to find your special way... after experiencing this powerful experience of birth you know you can successfully meet other challenges you will encounter in your life... the ability already exists in you and it will go on increasing...

And with this affirming knowledge you begin to return to normal awareness, to here, to this room... you can move your hands and feet a little... move your body gently... move your head gently from side to side... take a deep breath... and another breath... slowly open your eyes... and return at your pace to normal wakefulness and to full awareness... and to here and now.

53. Born Again

54. The Inner Vision

Category:
Strengthening resources

Who can benefit from this meditation?
People who are interested in allowing their body to rest and to focus on their vision.

Surrender

*Nothing can be done
at the moment,
Other than to accept
things as they are.
Take a break and focus
on your vision.
In the meantime, do nothing,
Other than wait till the
end of this period of
imbalance.*

Allow yourself to find a comfortable position... feel the contact of your body on the mattress or on the chair... close your eyes... pay attention to the sounds outside and those you can hear inside the room... allow the sounds to focus you on my voice... today you are going on a journey of growth and learning... and perhaps you are excited ahead of the journey... your subconscious is very wise and takes care of you, so you can loosen up knowing that it is doing its job in the best possible way... allow yourself to slowly and gradually get into a state of relaxation and calmness... to rest a little from everyday thoughts and activity and simply breathe deep... and listen...

Allow yourself to focus your attention on your feet... feel your toes... and your feet... let them rest... relax... to enter calm sleep... your attention slowly climbs and rises over the shins... the knees... the thighs... you are bringing balance and rest to your legs...

Your attention continues to rise across the pelvis... to the stomach cavity and the lower back... the serenity spreads gradually through all the internal organs... the heart... and your attention rises to the chest, to the upper back, passes the shoulder blades and the shoulders... moves towards the arms and reaches the hands... allow the shoulders and the hands that are so burdened during the day to rest... to gather renewed strength...

Your attention reaches the nape and the neck... and from it to the chin... to the mouth... your jaws are loose and at ease... calm serenity is sent to the nose and the cheeks... to the eyes... soft eyes... and to your hair... the head is calm and comfortable... it is a very pleasant feeling... simply allow yourself to rest... to sink further and further into a deep serenity... more and more...

Now your whole body is loose and relaxed... there is quiet and ease in every corner... and when your body is calm you can focus your attention on your vision: on your deepest desire... that stems from the depths of the heart... a hidden goal... a secret yearning... a need awaiting its hour, to be satisfied...

I will now be quiet for about two minutes to allow you to focus, serenely and calmly, on your deepest, most basic desire... on your vision... you will hear my voice again in about two minutes...

You are still at rest, you can return inside yourself to your vision, to the goal you set yourself... you understand that rest is a good time to have thoughts and ideas, to ponder yourself and your deepest aspirations... whenever you want, you will be able to loosen up and rest... to focus on your deepest desires... on your needs... knowing you can move in the right direction for you... to realize dreams... to follow the heart...

And it is now clear to you that from a state of serenity and calmness you are capable of connecting to your inner self... to the primary place inside you... at times things progress slowly, and there are periods when things happen more quickly... at the same time, things always move in a certain direction... and in your heart you know the direction... the destination... and as time passes you will be able to focus yourself more and more...

And with this good feeling and this important knowledge, you begin to return and feel your body... to wake it up slowly... slowly... gradually move your hands... and your feet... moisten your lips a little... gently open your eyes... relaxed eyes... at your own pace return to normal awareness and normal wakefulness, to here and now.

54. The Inner Vision

55. The Ocean of Abundance

Category:
Strengthening resources

Who can benefit from this meditation?
People who are interested in connecting to abundance and to attract abundance into their life.

Abundance

It is a delightful peak period,
A time of abundance.
You will be able
to realize yourself.
It is an opportunity
to discover yourself afresh.
Allow yourself
to enjoy the moment,
And to act while it lasts,
before it disappears.

Close your eyes and find a comfortable position... take a deep breath and allow your body to loosen up and rest... perhaps you can hear voices from outside... allow yourself to focus on my voice... feel how you allow yourself to relax... slowly, slowly... feel the contact of your body on the chair or on the mattress... feel how you connect to an inner place inside yourself... a quiet place... a safe place... a particular place where you know you have a lot of good things in your life... lots of happy moments... lot of love... you can remember them and celebrate them... it calms you... and allows you to rest... you can feel your heartbeats and they are so relaxing... and the ease in your whole body...

Imagine yourself standing on the shore of an enormous ocean... it is the ocean of abundance... you can see the horizon and the expanse of the ocean and be amazed by its size... allow yourself to listen to the sound of the waves breaking gently on the shore... to the splashing of the water... you are barefoot and feel the contact with the sand, or perhaps you are wearing beach sandals or flip-flops...

From afar you can hear the sounds of birds in flight... you can smell the fragrance of the sea and observe its colors... the sea allows you to experience a feeling of freedom...

The sound of the water splashing and the looking at the sea create a feeling of serenity in you... you look at the waves and feel that their rhythm is like the rhythm of your breath... you breathe and feel more and more relaxed... the air goes in and out just like the waves reaching the shore and returning, again and again...

You know it is an extraordinary ocean... an ocean in which all the earth's abundance exists... endless abundance... there is great abundance in our world, and it is available to everybody... every person can receive as much as he/she wants from the great store of abundance, and there will be enough for everybody... abundance is not just money. There is an abundance of love... of friends... of good feelings... of good relationships... anything that makes you happy can be the abundance in your life... and you are entitled to get the best...

The sense of abundance fills you with joy... you can choose a receptacle – a cup or golden goblet or large tub or pipe – and fill it with abundance from the ocean's waters... the abundance is intended to serve you and to assist you... you can use it to bring into your life things that you want... you can spoil yourself with things you like, knowing there is enough abundance in the world, and that you are worthy of everything you want... imagine filling the vessel with great abundance, more and more... connect to your strength and ability to bring this abundance into your life...

I will now be quiet for about two minutes to allow you to connect to the source of abundance and to feel how you will use the abundance that reaches you... you will hear my voice again in about two minutes...

And now, after connecting to the source of abundance and it has become part of you... of your life... you can think about what you should still do for yourself... what can you allow yourself so that you feel better... what things will you want to do for yourself with your abundance... if you feel you need a larger receptacle in order to collect more treasure from the sea of abundance, you can change the receptacle as you wish (wait a moment)...

You leave the enormous ocean, full of abundance... express your gratitude... as time passes the feeling you have that you are worthy of great abundance will get stronger... that the abundance you receive is intended for you, and it is within your ability to receive more and more things you need... the sea of abundance is very big and it contains enough for absolutely everybody...

As time passes you will strengthen your connection to abundance and summon to yourself more and more resources that will help you along any path you choose to go... the sea of abundance is always there for you... you can return to it at any time and receive more and more from it... the feeling of wellbeing and ease that abundance creates percolates through your whole body, from your feet to the top of your head... your heart fills with love for the wonders of the world... you feel expansive and strengthened... a feeling of satisfaction and ease...

And with this wonderful feeling, you are invited to begin slowly and gradually to return to here, to this room... and you begin to return... you can move your hands and feet a little... move your body gently... move your head gently from side to side... take a deep breath... and another breath... slowly open your eyes and return at your pace to normal wakefulness and to full awareness... and to here and now.

55. The Ocean of Abundance

56. The Market of Possibilities

Category:
Choosing direction

Who can benefit from this meditation?
People who have abundant possibilities and are interested in finding a way to make a choice.

The Wanderer

*This is a time to explore
new things,
And taste a little of each,
In order to decide what is right
for you.
Connect to yourself,
And check where this
journey is taking you.*

Allow yourself to find a comfortable position... you will be able to feel your body on the chair or on the mattress... relax your muscles slightly... slowly start to feel comfortable... it is a time of rest for you... for your body... a time that allows the head to get rid of the thoughts and to loosen up... let your thoughts dissolve like bright clouds in the sky that move with the wind, dissolve and disappear... you will be able to hear voices from outside and the music playing here in the room... allow yourself to focus on my voice... and feel how you become more and more comfortable from minute to minute...

Imagine yourself arriving at a nice, colorful market... this market has everything – colorful stalls... traders selling their wares... food that smells good... all sorts of clothes... household goods... colorful carpets... everything...

You walk through the market... aware of the noises going on around you... something in you remains calm amongst the tumult... you know that at the heart of the market there is an extraordinary section... which is where you want to get to...

You ask one of the hawkers which way to go to get to the possibilities market... he points to a path that is paved with stones of various colors... blue stones... green... red... orange and purple... you start walking along this colorful path towards the possibilities market...

You reach a small lane in the market and enter it... the possibilities market has a small, green gate, an age-old gate... you open the gate and go inside... music that you like is playing inside... you notice that there are fewer people here... there is a pleasant atmosphere in the possibilities market and you feel calm and relaxed... displayed here are all the possibilities available to you... and you are invited to choose...

You stroll among the stalls looking at the possibilities... there is an abundance of possibilities in every area: in the area of relationships... career... parenthood... leisure possibilities... studies... you can choose the area you are pondering about and examine the various possibilities that this wonderful market offers you... some are familiar to you... some are new and are only revealed to you now... there are always at least three possibilities... and usually even more... they appear before you one by one...

I will now be quiet for about two minutes for you to examine the various possibilities that the market offers in the sphere you have chosen... you will hear my voice again in about two minutes...

And now that you have considered the possibilities and looked at the stalls... you can choose the possibility you are interested in... or you can choose to allow yourself to wander around more and choose later... on the side you detect a stall you had not noticed until now... it is a stall with a scale... with it you can weigh up the advantages and disadvantages of each and every possibility before buying it... you can bring different possibilities from each stall and weigh them... in this way you can check for yourself which possibility is the best for you... you are aided by this stall and know that every decision you take will be the best one you can take now... and that after deciding you will be happy with your decision... (wait a minute).

You chose, you bought the best possibilities for yourself... you decide to return... you leave via the green gate... and make your way back to the big, main market... you go along the path of the colored stones that symbolize the range of possibilities... on your way, you come to a stall selling gem stones... and you choose the stone you like best... a stone that can confirm your choice of possibilities that suit you best... and only for you... that will allow you to find your way on the journey of unlimited possibilities... the journey of life...

You buy the stone and put it in your pocket... and you walk with it the whole way... with the new possibilities you purchased on the journey today, and when this stone is in your pocket, you have a good feeling... special...

And with this good feeling you begin to return to normal awareness to here, to this room... you can move your hands and feet a little... move your body gently... move your head gently from side to side... take a deep breath... and another breath... slowly open your eyes... return at your pace to normal wakefulness and to full awareness... and to here and now.

56. The Market of Possibilities

57. A Message from the Wind

Category:
Solving Problems

Who can benefit from this meditation?
People who are interested in refining their way of behaving and responding and still influence their lives.

Gentleness

*Just as the wind changes the
landscape very slowly,
So you can influence people
and situations
in a gentle way.
Take time for yourself,
To focus on your needs and to
arrange your thoughts,
Ahead of gradually
achieving your desires.*

Allow yourself to find a comfortable position... you will be able to feel your body on the chair or on the mattress... you are resting and slowly, slowly begin to experience a feeling of comfort... it is a time of rest for you... for your body... it is a time that allows the head to free itself a little from thoughts and to loosen up... you will hear voices from outside... allow yourself to focus on my voice... and feel how the calmness pervades you... you become more relaxed from moment to moment...

Imagine yourself sitting facing the sea... looking at the waves... the waves reach the shore... become white foam... and then retreat, go back... and come again... and retreat again... looking at the waves calms you... and you can hear the sounds of the water moving back and forth, coming and going...

You can feel the murmur of the wind on your face... there is wind at the sea... and it blows your hair lightly... you wonder if the wind helps the waves to reach the shore and to go back or if the water finds its own way... you observe nature's power of movement... the mighty power of the waves... the wind's mighty, yet gentle, power... you feel free, relaxed and loose... more and more comfortable...

The smell of salt rises in your nose... the good smell of the sea... you breathe in the pleasant air... it calms you. You like sitting and looking at the sea a lot... there are rocks near the shore... they are smooth and rounded, it seems the water and the wind make shapes of them... the water breaks over the rocks and rubs them a little each time… the wind spreads the sand that is produced… it sculpts the sand slowly in its gentle way…

You also feel your ability to influence people and situations in a gentle way… you feel the need to learn how to let things be what they are… just like the sea and the rocks and the water… to be themselves, and, at the same time, to influence… in a gentle manner… in a manner that helps them to progress with confidence and allows them to remain calm and serene…

Sometimes you want people to behave differently… for things to be as you want… like many people, you want things to be under your control… and when that does not happen, you feel disappointed… frustrated… though today you have the opportunity to learn ancient wisdom from the wind…

The wind is whispering something to you… something you can hardly hear… though you slowly begin to hear the words… to understand the meaning… the wind is telling you a secret, "I, too," says the wind, "can be very blustery, create storms that smash everything around them… and then it very hard to repair what I have wrought"…

And you continue to listen to the wind's wisdom, which impresses you… something in its airy voice calms you… "and I can also affect things differently, extremely gently… slowly, slowly… a little each time… here, I move sand from one place to another… gently pass over animals and people… for years, I gently abrade the edges of rocks… direct the flow of water from one place to another… I let things stay basically as they are, and each time cause a small change"…

"And sometimes," the wind continued, "we do not notice the little changes we effect… perhaps a little smile we smiled at someone… a gentle tap on the shoulder… a word said… we listened without commenting… without judging… we planted hope… this is our ability to create change gently in ourselves and in others"…

The wind finished speaking... and suddenly stopped blowing... you ponder the things the wind said and begin to remember all the tiny, delicate changes you have felt lately in your life or you felt in other people's lives... like grains of sand flying from one place to another... the little smiles and the delicate gestures now come to mind... perhaps some ideas arise, as well as thoughts about other changes you can make in your life...

I will now be quiet for about two minutes to allow you to ponder this... you will hear my voice again in about two minutes...

The wind starts blowing again gently around you... you feel as if it is massaging your back... your shoulder blades and your shoulders... a light shiver passes over your back... the wind is sending you pleasant, gentle energy that heals... comforts... calms... you thank it for sharing its ancient wisdom with you... and bid it farewell...

And with this new knowledge, you are invited to separate from the wind in the meantime and begin to make your way back to here, to this room... the new knowledge fills you with calmness, happiness and joy like you experienced now... you begin to return here... you can move your hands and feet a little... move your body gently... move your head gently from side to side... take a deep breath... and another breath... slowly open your eyes... and return at your pace to normal wakefulness and to full awareness... and to here and now.

57. A Message from the Wind

58. A Chat with a Good Friend

Category:
Strengthening resources

Who can benefit from this meditation?
People who need support and encouragement.

Encouragement

*At this time your powers of
encouragement are at their best.
You are invited to encourage
whoever needs you.
Real encouragement
from the heart,
Will influence people and
strengthen them.
Encouraging others will also
strengthen you.*

Allow yourself to find a comfortable position... close your eyes... listen to the voices outside and in the room... these voices help you to focus your attention on my voice... it is time for you to rest... allow yourself to relax your body... loosen up... free your head from thoughts... let your thoughts fly off far into the sky like a flock of birds... take a deep breath... and another one... slowly, slowly feel the serenity spread around your whole body...

Imagine yourself arriving at the home of a good friend of yours... it can be a friend you know... or an imaginary friend... an old friend from the past or perhaps a friend you always wanted to have... one who boosts you and you boost...

You knock on her/his door and he/she opens it with a broad smile... she invites you to come in... you go inside and sit down at the kitchen table... your friend offers you something to drink... you drink a drink that you like... there is a pleasant smell in the air... she asks you how you are... is interested to know what is happening with you... how you feel... sitting with her at the table creates a feeling of ease and calm in you... something about this friend and her home, you find pleasant... calms you...

And when you reply and begin to tell your story, you notice she listens to you intently... asks for more details... many of the things troubling you trouble her as well, or did in the past... she understands you... identifies with you... when you have finished chatting she says some things you find very encouraging... she thinks you will be able to cope with what happens to you...

Allow yourself to hear what your good friend is telling you... that she believes in you... that she has confidence in your ability... she encourages you in the area you are preoccupied with...

I will now be quiet for about two minutes to allow you to hear what she says... you will hear my voice again in about two minutes...

Your friend's words echo in you... you hear them again and again... and now your friend is telling you what she is going through... you listen closely to her... encourage her... you realize you are able to encourage her... to improve her mood... you do not judge her... you accept her as she is and allow her to feel good about herself... just as you felt she did for you... you feel how what you say makes her happy and it fill you with happiness...

Your friend now offers you a small box containing a present... you open the box and find in it a beautiful conch... you feel the conch and put it to your ear... you can hear the sound of the sea... it is a special conch... you can also hear words of encouragement from it... you are amazed and, at the same time, understand that the conch will remind you of your ability to encourage others... and of your ability to accept encouragement from others... you will always be able to find people whom you know are able to encourage you... those who accept you as you are... and genuinely want you to grow... and you should know that you can also encourage them... this is an important and good ability... and you can increase it as time passes... your ability to encourage and your ability to receive encouragement from others increases more and more...

Your friend tells you that the conch came from the lake of happiness... according to Chinese belief, the waters of this lake sparkle with joy under the sky... calm resides in the depths... the lake symbolizes inner and outer happiness... deep happiness that exists inside and the lighter type that comes from outside... you are charmed by the story and feel how you are filled with this happiness... the conch has brought happiness to you from the depths of the lake...

You place the conch close to your heart and fill up more and more with the special happiness... you thank your fiend for the chat and for the wonderful present she gave you... and you say goodbye to her in your own way... with a handshake or an embrace of perhaps a kiss... your friend invites you to come back to visit her... you take the conch with you... keeping it close to your heart, and go on your way...

And from your friend's home, with the feeling of happiness accompanying you... you begin to return slowly to here, to this room... to feel your body... you take a deep breath... and another... you can move your hands gently... and your feet... you open your eyes at your pace... and return to normal wakefulness... to full awareness... to here and now.

58. A Chat with a Good Friend

59. *The River*

Category:
Solving Problems

Who can benefit from this meditation?
People who are caught in a conflict between thought and feeling.

Reunion

There are times when you
can reunite things.
Even rivals can unite around
a common problem.
This is an opportunity to unify
the voices inside you,
To find your unique voice and
to listen to it.

Allow yourself to rest a little... to have a break from everyday matters... find a comfortable position... close your eyes and allow them to rest from all sights... and let your ears rest from all the voices and focus on my voice... feel the chair or mattress you are sitting or lying on... all your senses are resting now... relaxing more and more... your brain, responsible for thinking, is also comfortable... your heart, responsible for emotions, is comfortable... you feel calmer and calmer... and are ready to embark on a journey... a journey of the imagination... a journey on which anything can exist... anything can happen... and everything is safe and protected... allow yourself to embark on a special journey... wonderful and magical... a journey devoted entirely to your personal development...

Imagine yourself standing next to a wide river... it is formed by many tributaries... if you walk along its length, you will see how the tributaries lead into it and together create a large, swirling river... the river flows down... aware of its special path... carrying good, thirst-quenching water to the plants... to animals and people...

You observe the tributaries and streams coming onto the river and others coming out of it... you see that some simply leave and flow in other directions, and there are some that split and return... you feel that sometimes there are different voices in you... different desires... various needs... and this makes life difficult for you... you would like to unite the voices, the needs and the desires into one single clear voice that will help you to go in one direction... at the same time, you know that the various voices help you... guide you and allow you to be attentive to all the desires and urges inside you...

And like the river that branches out and joins up again, so it is with us, people, having various voices... often our heart wants something... and our head wants something different... and when we want to know how to advance we feel confused, stuck... as if the opposing forces make it difficult for us to advance...

Imagine yourself as a river... you will be able to examine what different tributaries there are in you... focus first on the main tributary: your head... firstly, you can thank it for everything it does for you... imagine it flowing and carrying water... the flow of the water is like the flow of thoughts... what thoughts cross your mind? What does your head want to advance? What is important to it? What does it feel? You can also ask your head what you can do for it... you can check with it if it feels your heart is flowing with it along the same course, or whether the heart is flowing along an opposing course?...

I will now be quiet for about two minutes to allow you to ponder this... you will hear my voice again in about two minutes...

Now you can turn to your heart... to the stream of your emotions... thank it for everything it does for you... after that you can ask it: What does it feel? What does it want? What does it want from you? Allow yourself to really discuss with your heart (wait a moment) what is its good intention for you? What would it want you to have? What would it want you to do? And what would it want to say to your head?

Now you can see if there are other tributaries of your river... are there other channels with opposing desires? conflicting intentions?... your strength will increase greatly... your river will flow better once you have created agreement and cooperation among the tributaries... among all the streams... allow yourself to unite them... reunion... a union in which each one will find its place... each of them: the head, the heart and perhaps other streams will know that their voice is heard amongst the swirl of the big, powerful river... and, at the same time, know how to cooperate in order for the whole flow to be united... significant... observe the tributaries in you: On what are they agreed? Cooperatively, where would they choose to flow together?

I will now be quiet for another minute to allow you to ponder this... you will be able to hear my voice again in a minute...

And you feel how the power of your river... your inner power... is increasing by the minute... it is increasing by virtue of your wonderful ability to talk to its various streams and tributaries... to listen to each one and create common ways of working... it is a great feeling and arouses in you a sense of new life... of progress... of a marvelous ability to create a flow... with flexibility... a flow that has direction... that has the ability to advance and to create change...

And with this wonderful feeling, and you are full of new strength... as new powers and old-new abilities have been awakened in you... you are invited to return... at a pace that suits you... to here, to this room... you slowly begin to return to normal wakefulness and normal awareness... to feel your body again... to move your hands a little... and your feet... open your eyes and return, at your own pace... to here and now.

59. The River

60. Setting Limits

Category:
Finding direction

Who can benefit from this meditation?
People who are interested in setting limits and finding a way that suits their needs.

Limits

Limits create order,
Whereas, when all
possibilities exist,
And all limits are removed,
You can get lost.
Hence you must judge
for yourself,
The limits you can set,
In order to do things
in a way that suits you.

Allow yourself to find a comfortable position... feel comfortable in every part of your body... and take a deep breath... feel the temperature in the room... allow yourself, slowly, slowly to relax... listen to the voices from outside... and the voices in the room... to the sounds of the music... let the music and my voice lead you to relaxation and rest... go inside yourself and loosen up... slowly, slowly... you can pay attention to your breathing... to the rhythm of your breathing... does the air come in and go out easily?... with every inhalation bring serenity and calmness to your body... with each exhalation release anything you don't need... stress, hassles, tension... again take a deep breath... change to normal breathing that is comfortable for you... paying attention to breathing calms you more and more...

Imagine yourself in a field on a clear morning... the grass is green and fresh and dewdrops sparkle on it... the field is wide and very big... you can see green carpets of various shades in every direction... above them a pale blue sky... the view is beautiful... a light breeze is blowing and you can feel its gentle contact with your face... it is very quiet around... being in nature, in a green spot like this, relaxes you... you find it pleasant...

And you can go in any direction you want... all possibilities are open to you... the field is wide and permits you to walk around in it... and you can't decide which way to go... which way to turn... you feel uncertain… where will these paths lead you, and what is hidden further along the side of this endless field?

You would prefer one clear path… a proper road… that you know where it leads… that is clear to you… when there are so many possibilities it is hard to know which way to turn… you choose a particular direction and begin to stride along it, just like that… you simply walk and enjoy walking in the lovely field… after a short time you notice a path that winds ahead of you… at first it is small and a little blurred… almost unnoticed… though it gradually turns into a real road…

You feel relieved when you notice that it has become a proper, clear path… and you think that perhaps this path leads to some place… somebody has been on it before and prepared it… you also understand that this path has a goal… some purpose… and you feel that the path you chose suits you… you continue to walk and the scenery changes… around you there are more and more trees and bushes… it is no longer the wide field you were in before… it also has fences marking the grazing areas of animals… you continue to walk… listening to the sounds of the cows and sheep around you… and at the side of the path you notice a goat pen…

There are fences around the path you are walking on… they form a sort of farm lots in a rural environment… the scene, which has become more settled, creates a more relaxed feeling in you… calmer… there is order in things, the proximity of other people makes you feel you are not alone… and the fencing creates clarity in you… where to walk and where not to walk…

You realize that this path reflects something in your life… you find it easier when things are clear… when there are limits that you set… limits for yourself and for other people… you find it easier when you define what suits you to do… what you want… coming from a deep connection to yourself… then, you clarify for yourself what you want and you say it in a way that your surrounding can understand exactly what your limits are: how much, for example, you are prepared to help... or do...

Sometimes there is a feeling that limits restrict... that they might reduce possibilities... at the same time, you know that limits prescribe order... clarify what is right and what is not... and in life, as on this path you are walking along today, it is easier to walk in the clearly-marked areas than to wander in a totally open field...

Now you are looking back at the open field... you remember that now and again you like being in a wide, open space, without limits... to be curious... to walk in a field where all paths are possible and it is possible to test all of them and see where they lead... there are times when the paved, fenced path suits you more... and there are periods when you yearn for the wide open spaces... for the open field... clarity and knowing the direction and the pleasure of exploring new, unfamiliar ways are just as important to you...

With this important insight, you can begin to return to normal awareness here, to this room... you can move your hands and feet a little... move your body gently... move your head gently from side to side... take a deep breath... and another breath... slowly open your eyes... and return at your pace to normal wakefulness and to normal awareness... to here and now.

60. Setting Limits

61. The Owl's Wisdom

Category:
Finding direction

Who can benefit from this meditation?
People who are interested in seeing things from above, in order to reach a deeper understanding of them.

Inner truth

Allow yourself to loosen up,
In order to gain real insight,
Into the matter that is preoccupying you.
The insight comes through understanding yourself and others,
And it can afford you some quiet.
Thanks to real insights,
You will also be able to pursue a vision.

Allow yourself to rest a little... to have a break from everyday matters... find a comfortable position... close your eyes and allow them to rest from all sights... and let your ears rest from all the voices and focus on my voice... feel the chair or mattress you are sitting or lying on... all your senses are resting now... relaxing more and more... your brain, responsible for thinking, is also comfortable... your heart, responsible for emotions, is comfortable... you feel calmer and calmer... and are ready to embark on a journey... a journey of the imagination... a journey on which anything can exist... anything can happen... and everything is safe and protected... allow yourself to embark on a special journey... wonderful and magical... a journey devoted entirely to your personal development...

Imagine yourself standing at the foot of a big tree... this is an age-old tree and with roots planted deep into the ground... its trunk is thick and its branches splay out in all directions... it is large and very sturdy... this tree instills a feeling of serenity and security in you... you see how it connects heaven and earth... a simple, clear connection... next to it you feel like it... your feet are planted on the ground and your head is up, towards the sky...

You hear sounds from the tree's branches... and notice an owl perched on one of the branches... you have never seen this type of owl... it is particularly big... and you hear it calling you... it invites you to join it on a journey... a journey full of insights... insights that only wise owls have...

The large owl comes down from the tree and stands next to you... you realize it is offering you to climb onto its back... you hesitate a little, then look at it and know that you can trust it... you climb onto its back and join it for a journey... the sky is clear and a pleasant breeze caresses your face when the owl takes off and goes on its way... you are sitting on its back and feel comfortable and safe... ready for flight...

From the owl's point of view you can see things differently... it takes you over your house... you can see what is happening in it like a spectator... as if you are inside the house yet observing from the side... when you are on the owl up high you view yourself... how you behave... what you say... what your thoughts are... what your emotions are...

You look at yourself from the perspective of the owl for a whole day... you see yourself getting up in the morning... you see what you do and where you go... and in this way you view your activities all day... until you go to sleep...

I will now be quiet for about three minutes in which you can view from above what is happening in your life during a whole day... you can gain insights about the way in which you conduct yourself... what would you like to change and what would you like to leave as it is... you will hear my voice again in about three minutes...

You observed yourself during a whole day... you gained new insights into yourself... they enable you to understand things differently – which behavior patterns you want to change... and what you want to keep...

The big owl continues to fly towards the tree from which you began the journey... you get off its back and it whispers something in your ear... allow yourself to receive a message from the owl's wisdom... (wait a moment)

Keep the message you received with you... you thank the owl for the journey, bid it farewell and go on your way... the owl returns to its branch on the tree... to its morning sleep... and you begin to return here knowing that you can always return to the owl, go on another journey and gain more insights from its great wisdom...

And with this heartening knowledge you begin to return and feel your body... to arouse it slowly... slowly... gradually move your hands... and feet... gently open your eyes... serene eyes... and return at your pace to normal wakefulness and full awareness... to here and now.

61. The Owl's Wisdom

62. Tidying the Room

Category:
Solving Problems

Who can benefit from this meditation?
People who are interested to put certain things in their lives in order, ahead of change.

Caution

*Big things are not going to advance now,
So we will use the time to deal with small things – details.
Thoroughly and humbly carry out all the routine errands.
You can expect success at the end of this period.*

Allow yourself to find a comfortable position and close your eyes... perhaps you can hear voices outside or in the room... these voices help you to focus your thoughts, very slowly, on all parts of your body... allow yourself to focus your attention on your head... feel how comfortable the head is and how pleasant it feels... sense how it feels inside it... it is pleasant to give the head attention... now you can travel with your attention over the whole body... to the feet, slowly and gently... feel how this trip relaxes you more and more... and when you reach the feet you feel serene and calm... more and more...

Imagine you are entering a room... the room is a little dark... and not really ventilated... and not tidy... there are too many things in it, spread all around the room... they create a feeling of overload... of lack of clarity... it is hard to use these things when they are in such a mess... today you have a chance to create order in this room... perhaps the room is familiar to you in your home or perhaps in another house... perhaps this room has just been created in your imagination...

Maybe you sometimes feel that you are overloaded... with thoughts... with emotions that flood you... with activity... perhaps your head is busy and loaded with too many different details... and you find it difficult to be efficient... to do things properly... your head is like this disordered room... you know that the moment you impose order on the things... the moment you decide what is important and what is not... you will clear space for relaxation... for order in your thinking... for inner quiet... for balance...

You begin to sort out the room... first, you take everything out... feel and touch them... look at them... some of them remind you of things from the past... happy events, or events you would rather forget... lots of memories are concealed in the items that have piled up over time... and maybe that is why it is not easy for you to take them out of the room... nevertheless, you understand that this is the time... you can expect some easing and serenity when everything is in order, clean and organized... after you have dispensed with things you no longer need... you know this is an opportunity for you to change things that you have wanted to change for a very long time... you take all the things you have taken out of the room and begin to arrange them in groups... what is needed and what is not... what is old and can be discarded and what you would like to keep... what is important and what is less important...

Before putting things back, you clean the cupboards in the room... and the room itself... the smell of the cleaning relaxes you and creates a feeling of renewal in you... for each piece you plan a suitable place... and how to arrange each item in its place... you begin to feel better because you understand that soon the place will be neat and tidy... and you understand that in your life too, as well as in your head overburdened with thoughts, you can impose order...

You arrange the items according to subjects... according to groups... and each thing has a place... and you throw out a lot of things because you realize you do not need them any longer... you can let them go now... everything you throw out clears a space... space that can remain empty... or be filled with new things that you choose... that you really want...

You have finished tidying the room just the way you like... you look at it and simply cannot believe your eyes... it is so pleasant and so nice... you inhale the good smell... you can find exactly the item you are looking for... and enjoy the things you have collected for your life... there is room for "everything"... and it really relaxes you...

You have significantly advanced something you have wanted to advance for a long time... you understand that focus and putting the house in order... and your head... and your heart... can serve as a basis for continuing... for creating a significant change in your life... to move you closer and closer to the life you want to be living... as you would like to experience... you now feel that it is possible and this makes you very happy...

And with the feelings of vitality and happiness... you begin to return to normal wakefulness, to here, to this room... you can move your hands and feet a little... move your body gently... move your head gently from side to side... take a deep breath... and another breath... slowly open your eyes and return at your pace to normal wakefulness and to full awareness... and to here and now.

62. Tidying the Room

63. Beyond the Peak

Category:
Finding direction

Who can benefit from this meditation?
People who successfully reach the end of a project/activity, and are starting again.

After the end

Every peak, however magnificent,
Prepares us for the next stage,
Which is like being reborn
(unfamiliar).
Allow yourself to enjoy the peak
you reached,
Though do not for a moment
be either euphoric
of apathetic,
About the future.

Allow yourself find a comfortable position and take a deep breath... and another breath... you will be able to notice your breathing... is it fast or slow?... does it move easily of does it encounter a difficulty in a particular place in your body?... pay attention to the flow of air from outside into the body and from the body back outside... and pay attention to how the progress of your breathing allows you to relax slowly, slowly... we sometimes forget to breathe in the fast pace of everyday life... for you this is an opportunity to breathe more deeply, to breathe comfortably and enable you to rest... to let go... allow your breathing to take you deep into yourself... to the most basic experience of existence... to breathing... to the wonderful ability of the body to nourish itself with oxygen all the time... and you take a breath and another breath... and permit yourself calm... it increases with each breath... and you are completely comfortable...

Imagine yourself to be standing on the peak of a mountain... it is a high mountain... you made a great effort to reach it, and now you are standing at the top... and looking around you... it is a very pleasant day and a delightful sun shines... the visibility is good and from the mountain peak you can see the valleys around, the lower peaks... the air is pleasant on your face, a light breeze is blowing...

You are happy to be on this peak... you reached it... you finally did it... a pleasant feeling of success pervades you... it is so good to reach a place you have been looking forward to reaching... how beautiful the view is from the peak...

A pleasant, refreshing light envelopes you in quiet and calm... the peak allows you to rest... to ponder the journey you have made... and the journeys still ahead of you... and at the same time, to rest... to let go the thoughts and simply be... a feeling of simple joy fills your heart... you can breathe deeply into this feeling... it is a wonderful feeling...

You look with satisfaction at the way you have come to get here... you made an effort and you realized a dream... a dream you have aspired to for a long time... and now there is a moment in which you look around and wonder which way to go... at the peak... even though it is pleasant, you cannot stay forever... you reached the top of the mountain, and now the time has arrived to continue walking...

A new period in your life is beginning now... like being born again... it is a different period... a new period is about to begin and you are excited by the range of possibilities before you... from the range of new possibilities... at the same time, you feel confused... in what direction should I proceed?... am I interested to begin conquering another, higher peak?... or to rest a little?... should I allow myself to get used to a new routine?...

After a short time, and after you have inhaled the pure, refreshing peak air... you understand that it is time to begin to go down... you lock the wonderful feelings of the success in your heart and you know that this is the moment to continue on your way... to begin to descend from this peak... you get up and begin to descend... taking care not to slip... you go down slowly and gradually from the mountain and look around you... nature's cyclicality creates ups and downs... a peak and the return to routine... you know that the descent now is the start of a new path... and you feel something is changing...

You descend while paying attention to your steps... to the slope... you go down through mist and at times can hardly see the path... you feel the mist is like your feeling... a lack of clarity with regard to the direction you are going in now... the mist continues and you walk carefully... every now and again you stop to check the path... where does it lead? Perhaps you are scared of falling to the bottom, though a sense of confidence in your ability to find the path envelopes you... and slowly and gradually the mist dissipates and the sky clears...

As you come through the mist you see a breath-taking sight... right beside the mountain you see a beautiful rainbow spread in the sky before you... a rainbow in an array of colors: red, orange, yellow, green, blue... the rainbow extends in front of you like a bridge... you go over it, through all the colors... you feel as if the colors are accompanying you on your way... they help you choose the right way after the peak... to understand where it leads... what new learning it permits... you cross the rainbow and are filled with its strength... filled with the good energy of a new beginning... with a sense of being grateful for the long way you have come and in anticipation of what lies ahead... and you inhale the colorful, healing energy of the rainbow... and know that you will find the right, good road for you...

As time passes this will become clearer... as time passes new directions open up and you will be able to choose the right direction for you... and with this wonderful feeling you begin slowly and gradually to return to here, to this room... and you begin to return to here... you can move your hands and feet a little... move your body gently... move your head gently from side to side... take a deep breath... and another breath... slowly open your eyes... and return at your pace to normal wakefulness and to full awareness... and to here and now.

63. Beyond the Peak

64. On the Mountainside

Category:
Solving Problems

Who can benefit from this meditation?
People who are about to complete a period/project/activity in a particular field and are in the midst of the final stages.

Before finishing

*You have been on your way for some time,
And you do it well and consistently.
Only a few steps remain
to the peak.
Perhaps you are afraid to get
to the top -
To end a period and begin a
new period,
Yet you are capable of it!
Take a breath and stride out,
joyfully, towards the peak.*

Allow yourself find a comfortable position and take a deep breath... and another breath... you will be able to notice your breathing... is it fast or slow?... does it move easily or does it encounter a difficulty in a particular place in your body?... pay attention to the flow of air from outside into the body and from the body back outside... and pay attention to how the progress of your breathing allows you to relax slowly, slowly... we sometimes forget to breathe in the fast pace of everyday life... for you this is an opportunity to breathe more deeply, to breathe comfortably and enable you to rest... to let go... allow your breathing to take you deep into yourself... to the most basic experience of existence... to breathing... to the wonderful ability of the body to nourish itself with oxygen all the time... and you take a breath and another breath... and permit yourself calm... it increases with each breath... and you are completely relaxed...

Life holds ups and downs for us: high mountains with peaks like dreams... followed by valleys... descent and then ascent again... in your life too there have been inclines that you scaled successfully to reach the peak and slopes that you descended... now you can rest in the knowledge that you will cope successfully with every situation that arises on your way...

Imagine yourself to be standing on a mountainside on a sunny winter day... a good sun warms you... you look around you... above you there are soft, calming clouds in the sly... you look at the mountain... the smells of winter's end reach your nose... you enjoy the fragrances of the flowers... a beautiful butterfly passes you by... you hear the delicate murmur of the flapping of its wings... and feel its flutter on your face... you feel comfortable and safe...

Today you are due to reach the top of the mountain... you know you care capable of it, because you have already been climbing up the mountainside for some time... you have the ability to continue and to persist on this journey and to reach the peak... the peak already seems within easy reach... and you begin to climb...

You can hear the sound of autumn leaves under your feet... you can feel the pleasant breeze on your face as you walk... you think about the climb ahead of you... it is likely to seem difficult to you... perhaps you are thinking about the peak itself... what it holds for you... what you will be able to see from it that you have not already seen... perhaps you are a little anxious about reaching it... in case you lose something when you reach the peak... and perhaps not...

Sometimes the peak seems jagged and sharp... you wonder if you will be there alone... sometimes it seems a little threatening because something will change in your life the moment you reach it... at the same time, you very much want to reach the peak... you have been waiting for this for a long time... and you sense that the air at the peak will do you good...

You continue to climb... the climb gets harder and harder... though you are able to continue to persevere... you continue to climb... one step after another... the calm view around you calms you... allows you to continue moving... to continue to walk... to breathe the air, that has become purer and purer... on your way you enter a clump of trees... and it is a little difficult to see where you are supposed to go in it... you clear your way through the trees... you slowly find the path and leave the clump of trees...

You stop to rest for a moment... you take a deep breath... the rest allows you to look back... you have come a very long way... allow yourself to remember your activity... your successes along the way... what has brought you this far... throughout the whole way you had an objective in mind... and now that you are very near the peak, you feel that the objective will soon be achieved... you feel excitement beating in your chest... excitement ahead of the peak... achieving the objective...

And now you can see the peak above you and the sound of birds can be heard as if they are singing just for you... the birds are singing a song you know, and like to accompany you to the beautiful peak... you look at the view... and then take a particularly long breath and take the last steps... perhaps they seem difficult and, at the same time, to your surprise, you simply skip to it... to the peak... lightly...

Now you are standing and looking at the view... it is a strikingly beautiful view... below you is a wonderful valley... bushes, trees and grass color it green... a blue river cuts across the green... from where you are standing now you can see things you had perhaps not noticed before... a deer is standing on the mountainside... an eagle glides above you... the sky is an enchanting light blue...

The peak air is pleasant... an light breeze caresses your face... and creates a good feeling... a feeling that something has ended... a chapter of your life has passed... and something new is about to begin... and you are excited... excited to know that you have done the whole trip... and reached this point under your own steam... it is a wonderful feeling...

Breathe this feeling into your body... feel the satisfaction of getting here... and from here you can begin to return gradually and slowly to here, to this room... and you begin to return to here... you can move your hands and feet a little... move your body gently... move your head gently from side to side... take a deep breath... and another breath... slowly open your eyes... and return at your pace to normal wakefulness and to full awareness... to here and now.

64. On the Mountainside

TABLE of meditations by type and purpose

Meditations to the Past

The name of the meditation	The name of the card	Who can benefit from this meditation?	The number of the card	The number of the page
Gratitude	Many Assets	People who are grateful for the abundance they have and wish to summon additional abundance into their lives.	14	78
A Letter from the Inner Child	Continuity	People who are interested in recalling pleasant, affirming memories from their childhood, and to gain strength from them.	32	152
The Success Ball	Gathering	People who are interested to remember the successes in their lives, and to draw strength from them to continue and succeed.	45	204
The Room of Strength	Great Strength	People who are interested in recalling their inner strengths and to be assisted by them on the way ahead.	34	160
A Message from Childhood	Ascent	People who want to remember pleasant things from their childhood.	46	208

Meditations to the Future

The name of the meditation	The name of the card	Who can benefit from this meditation?	The number of the card	The number of the page
Meet Your Future Self	Conduct	People who are interested in gaining insights from their future selves in order to be sure of their next step.	10	62
The Bus of the Future	Change	People who are interested in using the tools they have collected along the way and look to the future.	49	220
The Display Window	Basic Change	People who are interested in changing and to see the change in their life.	21	108
The Puzzle of My Life	Disintegration	People who feel that their life is coming apart and are interested to create a complete picture of reality.	23	116
The Tribe	The Family	People who seek their destiny, their role in society.	37	172
The Plate of Stones	Cosmic Order	People who want to create a clear scale of values in their life in order to live in harmony.	50	224

Meditations to Strengthening Resources

The name of the meditation	The name of the card	Who can benefit from this meditation?	The number of the card	The number of the page
Sprouting	Difficult Beginnings	Whoever is experiencing uncertainty, fear and excitement on their way to their new path.	3	34
The Subway	Calculated Waiting	For anybody who is forced to wait for something that cannot possibly happen immediately.	5	42
Baking Bread	Restraint	People who are attempting processes of change and creativity and are too hasty to see them through.	9	58
The Colors of Life	Community	People who are interested in improving their ability to accept somebody who is different and to create a community that operates collaboratively.	13	74
Pamper Yourself Day	Enthusiasm	People who need a break and to be pampered a bit.	16	88
An Ancient Chinese Saying	Progress	People who need encouragement and a message of progress and success.	19	100
The Hot Air Balloon	A Moment of Grace	People who are interested to travel to places they have dreamed of getting to.	22	112

The Spring of Calmness	Innocence	People who are interested in loosening control and allow themselves to be in the here and now.	25	124
Energy	Potential Energy	People who feel the need to be charged with new energy.	26	128
Diving Deep	Danger	People who are interested to delve into the depths of their soul.	29	140
Gliding in a Boat	Obstacle	People who encounter obstacles in their way and are interested in strengthening their ability to cope with them.	39	180
The Ocean of Abundance	Abundance	People who are interested in connecting to abundance and to attract abundance into their life.	55	244
A Chat with a Good Friend	Encouragement	People who need support and encouragement.	58	256
The Magnet	Attraction	People who are interested in attracting into their lives the things they want most, and are most appropriate.	31	148
Inner Light	Progress	People who are interested in gaining strength from their inner light.	35	164
The Well	The Source	People who are interested in connecting to their source.	48	216

Connecting to the Light	Hardship	People who are in difficulty and need resources to cope.	47	212
The Inner Vision	Surrender	People who are interested in allowing their body to rest and to focus on their vision.	54	240
Born Again	Development	People who feel they want to change, develop, grow and reveal themselves.	53	236
The Mountain	Stopping	People who are interested in looking at their life and do a soul-search of the past, the present and the future.	52	232

Mediations for Solving Problems

The name of the meditation	The name of the card	Who can benefit from this meditation?	The number of the card	The number of the page
Celestial Inspiration	The Power of Creation	Whoever wants to connect with the power of creation within him/herself and magnify it.	1	26
Mother Earth	The Receptive	Whoever wants to get pregnant and/or connect with her sense of motherhood, for Whoever wants to connect with her tender, feminine side and to allow things to develop on their own.	2	30
The Dove of Peace	Conflict	For anybody who is experiencing anger towards someone or is involved in a conflict or argument and wants to examine the situation in order to arrive at a solution.	6	46
The Ant Nest	United Force	People seeking to increase their ability to achieve goals through team work and unifying forces.	7	50
Improving Relationship with a Spouse	Unity	People looking for a relationship and people looking to improve their relationship, as well as people who want to raise a family.	8	54
Picking the Fruit	Peace	People who want to see themselves succeeding, especially those who have experienced fear of success.	11	66

Before the Snow Melts	Stagnation	People who feel stuck or not sufficiently active and are interested in experiencing the growth and ripening that is occurring beneath the surface.	12	70
Hills of Moderation	Humility	People who want to deal calmly with their surroundings.	15	82
The Frogs' Song	Repair	People who feel that an aspect of their life has been neglected and they want to do something about it.	18	96
The Kingdom of Good Nutrition	Nutrition	People who are interested in eating while paying attention to their body.	27	132
The Chore Sack	Too Much	People who are very busy and bothered and are looking for a bit of quiet and tranquility.	28	136
Shared Fire	Synergy	People who are interested in initiating collaborations.	30	144
Growing Towards the Light	Criticism	People contending with criticism.	36	168
The Water Pail	Release	People who are interested to release certain things from their lives to clear space for new things.	40	184
Weeding the Garden	Temptation	People who need to be cleansed and freed of the old and are interested to grow the new in their lives.	44	200

The Thought Box	Contradiction	People who are interested in strengthening their ability to think positively.	38	176
Between Tides	Reduction	People whose are going through a difficult period in their lives and want to change the situation, to move from low to high tide.	41	188
Tidying the Room	Caution	People who are interested to put certain things in their lives in order, ahead of change.	62	272
The Calm after the Storm	Turbulence	People who have undergone a significant change or been through a difficult period and are now beginning a new period.	51	228
The River	Reunion	People who are caught in a conflict between thought and feeling.	59	260
A Message from the Wind	Gentleness	People who are interested in refining their way of behaving and responding and still influence their lives.	57	252
On the Mountainside	Before Finishing	People who are about to complete a period/project/activity in a particular field and are in the midst of the final stages.	64	280

Meditations of Finding Direction

The name of the meditation	The name of the card	Who can benefit from this meditation?	The number of the card	The number of the page
The Cave Story	Inexperience	People who are interested in developing new coping strategies and in learning how to request and accept help from others.	4	38
Simple Flow	Adaptation	People who are want to loosen control and to go with the flow, to be like water.	17	92
Journey with the Wind	Contemplating	People who are need a moment of contemplation in order to look at their life differently.	20	104
New Growth	Turning Point	People who have blossomed in a particular area and are beginning a new journey of learning.	24	120
Time to Retreat	Retreat	People who are following a certain path and realize they have to retreat and follow a different path – to make a change.	33	156
The Crossroad	Decisiveness	People who are in the process of deciding and are struggling to choose.	43	196

The Emotions Compass	Benefit	People who are interested to connect to their heart's compass and so find the right direction for themselves.	42	192
Setting Limits	Limits	People who are interested in setting limits and find a way that suits their needs.	60	264
The Market of Possibilities	The Wanderer	People who have abundant possibilities and are interested in finding a way to make a choice.	56	248
The Owl's Wisdom	Inner Truth	People who are interested to see things from above, in order to reach a deeper understanding of them.	61	268
Beyond the Peak	After the End	People who successfully reach the end of a project/activity, and are starting again.	63	276

Bibliography

Ben-Shahar, T. (2008) Happier, Learn the Secrets of Daily Joy and Lasting Fulfillment, Matar Books

Gabbai, E. (2008) *Shikufim* cards (Hebrew) – Pictures of Inner Reflection

Graham, H. (1996) Guided Imagination, Or-Am Publishing

Hay, L. (1994) You Can Heal Your Life, Or-Am Publishing

Hecht, Y. (2009) Democratic Education – The Beginning of a Story, Updated Version, The Institute of Democratic Education

Honore, K. (2004) In Praise of Slow – Hebrew Version, Kinneret, Zmorra-Bitan, Dvir

Osho, Osho Zen Tarot, Gal Publishing

Weisman, N. (1983) I Ching (Hebrew translation), Astrolog Publishing

Wing, R.L. (1979) The I Ching Workbook, Mirkam Publishing

Retter, D.A. (1998) Communication with the Subconscious (Hebrew), Retter Publications

Retter, D.A. Change Begins with Imagination – workbook (Hebrew) first year students, Retter Publications

Retter, D.A. Change Begins with Imagination – workbook (Hebrew) second year students, Retter Publications

For more information about Ella Gabbai's products
you are invited to visit her website:
www.shikufim.info

She invites you to share your experiences,
comments or ideas about book:
Ella@shikufim.info

Ella Gabbai can also be reached by telephone:
(Israel) (0)50 - 686-6033

www.ingramcontent.com/pod-product-compliance
Lightning Source LLC
Chambersburg PA
CBHW071143160426
43196CB00011B/1999